Vital:
An Exercise in Practical Theology for Australian Churches

Ian Hussey

Anne Klose

Published by Morling Press,
Macquarie Park, Sydney Australia 2113

MORLING
PRESS

© Ian Hussy, Anne Klose 2023

The publication is copyright. Other than for the purpose of study and subject to the conditions of the Copyright Act, no part of it in any form or by any means (electronic, mechanical, micro-copying, photocopying or otherwise) may be reproduced, stored in a retrieval system or transmitted without the permission of the publisher.

ISBN 978-0-6454927-6-7

Cover and internal design by Impressum
www.impressum.com.au

All Scripture quotations, unless otherwise indicated, are taken from the Holy Bible New International Version. Copyright 1979 by Biblica, Inc. Used by permission. All rights reserved worldwide.

What a gift this book is to the Australian Church – good solid theology applied to ministry in a really practical way! The authors have done their theology well, reflecting on the scriptures, wisdom and praxis, and applied it to help churches grow in effective ministry practice for God's Kingdom. It will multiply the usefulness of the NCLS as a tool to grow our churches. I can't wait to use it with my ministers in Tasmania.

The Right Rev Dr Richard Condie
Bishop of Tasmania

This great new book by Ian Hussey and Anne Klose lives up to its name in every way. It guides church leaders through discussion of vital ingredients of a healthy church based on NCLS research and solid theology. This is practical theology at its best and most practical. Every church's leaders would benefit from a close and group-oriented study of this book.

Associate Professor Jon Newton
Alphacrucis College

In *Vital*, the authors offer an exercise in practical theology for local churches. They paint a beautiful vision of the Kingdom of God and bring it into dialogue with contemporary reality - which is practical, grounded, concrete, local and messy. I am delighted that Ian and Anne have drawn on the empirical research on models of church vitality that I have invested in over past decades. I am even more delighted that their aim is to help local church leadership translate these insights into practice for the sake of God's kingdom.

Dr Ruth Powell
Director, NCLS Research

Instead of offering quick-fix solutions, the authors of *Vital: An Exercise in Practical Theology* provide a process to assist church leaders to determine how to grow a kingdom-shaped church. Surveys such as NCLS have been useful as church health checks but often leaders have not known what to do next. Pastors from every type and size of church will find this book invaluable in making informed choices about future directions. An easy to read book that will inspire hope and confidence.

Rev Canon Dr Richard Trist
Senior Lecturer in Pastoral Theology, Ridley College

In Australia where secularisation continues to increase and church expansion is challenging for many, this book arrives! Hussey and Klose, through well founded and thoughtful research, provide for churches and their leadership a practically focused book to develop godly and important foundations for their community's life and health. This book will become a key text for both Australian and global contexts in establishing the factors that are vital for a healthy and godly church, and their growth and expansion. Enjoy the reflective questions provided for churches to work through, be encouraged by its practical suggestions, and most of all enhanced by its well considered theological basis and thought. This is truly a must read.

Rev Dr Keith Mitchell
Senior Lecturer Pastoral and Practical Studies, Morling College

This is the book I wish I had written to serve churches! It beautifully straddles theology, engagement with data and practice. The book is just the right length for busy church members, and so while it cannot explore in-depth every nuance of vitality it is based on the National Church Life Survey measures of church vitality; framing each dimension within God's unfolding plan of Biblical theology, and by distilling a vast scope of literature it offers sensible proposals that call for simple and contextually nuanced action. *Vital* should be on every church council's, eldership, or deacon's activity list for this year.

Rev Archie Poulos
Head, Ministry Department, Moore Theological College
Director, the Centre for Ministry Development

This book is not gold – it's better than that, it's a treasure map. If you like reading for the sake of reading, it will be just one more book about churches. But if you're reading for the real action and adventure of serving and representing Jesus on the ground, in practice, as a local church – then you'll find it valuable indeed. A church leadership team that works through *Vital* together will profit in all the ways that matter. Drawn from Scripture, careful research and real leadership experience - take this treasure map and see where it leads!

Rev Andrew Turner
Director of Crossover for Australian Baptist Ministries

Contents

Introduction 1

Chapter 1: Kingdom Aligned Vision 15

Chapter 2: Strong Community 33

Chapter 3: Outward Focus 49

Chapter 4: Empowering Leadership 67

Chapter 5: Vibrant Faith 85

Chapter 6: Inspiring Worship 105

Chapter 7: Intentional Discipleship 121

Chapter 8: Caring for the Young 143

Chapter 9: Generous Giving 163

Conclusion 181

Appendix 1 – Supplementary Questions............................. 185

Appendix 2 – What is "Vibrant" Faith? 199

About the Authors 203

Introduction

Practical Theology?

An oxymoron is a figure of speech in which two words are put together in an unexpected way. One of the most famous oxymorons is found in the title of Simon and Garfunkel's song, "The Sound of Silence." "True Lies," a movie starring Arnold Schwarzenegger is an oxymoron (not Arnold, the movie). But we use them quite commonly in everyday life. For example, "act naturally," "modern history," "minor miracle," and "small crowd" are things that we might all have said. Some oxymorons, like "Microsoft Works" and "airline food," are just funny, whilst others, like "civil war" and "friendly fire" represent more tragic realities.

For many of us in church leadership, putting theology and the practicalities of faith and church together may well seem like an oxymoron. Putting the words "practical" and "theology" in the same sentence, let alone combining them to form a noun (or, as we will come to see, verb) will seem unnecessary for some and even unpalatable for others. But if such a perception is true, it is a disaster for the church.

David Smith diagnoses two problems when it comes to theology and church life: blind theology and blind praxis.[1] Blind theology is what happens when theology is done without consideration of the practical realities of the church it should be serving. Blind praxis is what happens when the Church acts without consideration of theology. In both scenarios the Church is cut adrift from the crucial theological insights it needs to function as God intends, instead often resorting to pragmatism ("It worked for the church down the road so it might work for us") or traditionalism ("That's just the way we do things around here.")

Our aim in this book is to invite you into the faithful and fruitful integration of God's purposes for our local churches (theology) and the practical know-how of living this out (praxis). This is *Practical Theology*, and you will notice that we have capitalised the term. We do this to highlight that Practical Theology, at least in the way we are talking about it in this book, is not just about the practical skills associated with pastoral ministry like visitation, preaching and church administration, but is a sub discipline of theology alongside Systematic Theology and Biblical Theology.

Woodward et al. define "Practical Theology" as "a place where religious belief, tradition, and practice meets contemporary experiences, questions, and actions and conducts a dialogue that is mutually enriching, intellectually critical, and practically transforming."[2] As such, Practical Theology seeks to bridge the gap between theology and action. It is this definition of Practical Theology we will adopt for this book and, as you'll discover, we don't just want you to read about it but to practise it for yourselves.

And the guiding motif for our exercise in Practical Theology for your local church will be the kingdom of God.

Practical Theology for the Kingdom of God

When Jesus was on earth, what was the thing he most talked about? Most of you won't be surprised to hear that it was the kingdom of God. In both his words and actions Jesus was all about the gospel of the kingdom which, in him, was breaking out in revolutionary ways. Mark introduces the ministry of Jesus in the following way:

> [14] After John was put in prison, Jesus went into Galilee, proclaiming the good news (gospel) of God.[15] "The time has come," he said. "The kingdom of God has come near. Repent and believe the good news (gospel)!"

The gospel (good news) that Jesus proclaimed was that the kingdom of God had arrived and that the fitting response was repentance and belief.

As you'll see as you read on, while Practical Theology draws on many resources, God and his purposes must always be front and centre. So, right at the beginning of this book, we want to set out our vision of what it means for local churches to play their part in God's great story: the story which holds together and makes sense of all that we believe and, in Christ, seek to accomplish. And, in following Scripture's lead, we have chosen to frame this in terms of God's kingdom.

In Scripture we learn, firstly, that God is king of the whole universe: creation is, as Nicholas Perrin reminds us, "a sovereign act," by which God moves autonomously, powerfully and personally.[3] Israel was his own "treasured possession," called to be a "priestly kingdom," and yet the context for this was and remained that "the whole earth is mine" (Exod 19:5-6). As the psalmist exults to tell it:

> [1] Clap your hands, all you nations;
>   shout to God with cries of joy.
> [2] For the LORD Most High is awesome,
>   the great King over all the earth.
> [3] He subdued nations under us,
>   peoples under our feet.
> [4] He chose our inheritance for us,
>   the pride of Jacob, whom he loved.
> [5] God has ascended amid shouts of joy,
>   the LORD amid the sounding of trumpets.
> [6] Sing praises to God, sing praises;
>   sing praises to our King, sing praises.
> [7] For God is the King of all the earth;
>   sing to him a psalm of praise.
> [8] God reigns over the nations;
>   God is seated on his holy throne.
> [9] The nobles of the nations assemble
>   as the people of the God of Abraham,
> for the kings of the earth belong to God;
>   he is greatly exalted. (Psalm 47)

The tragedy of humanity's rebellion has not, cannot, change the fact of God's kingship. Sin is a form of attempted secessionism which, in God's time, will be laid bare before the world as a treacherous and death-dealing exercise in futility.

God's eternal and sovereign answer to this problem came with the establishment of a kingdom pattern: "God's people, in God's place, under God's rule."[4] In his steadfast love, God revealed this pattern through his covenants: kingdom treaties made with his people for his kingdom purposes. At the forefront of these purposes was blessing for Israel and, through Israel, the establishment of blessing for "all the families of the earth" (Gen 12:1b-3).[5] This kingdom pattern played out again and again through Israel's exodus from Egypt and establishment in the promised land, in glimpses of the true king and kingdom under David, and through exile and return. Yet, by Jesus' time, the kind of kingdom blessing promised to Abraham remained unfulfilled as God's people struggled under the oppressive yoke of yet another godless ruler and empire in a long line of godless rulers and empires.

For some Jews of the New Testament era, this oppression was Israel's most obvious problem, and their response was to address it directly through the violent overthrow of their Roman oppressors. But Jesus diagnosed and treated the far deadlier and more deeply rooted issue of rebellious sin. God's kingdom would finally be established, not through violence or even the Pharisee's outward show of keeping the law, but by God's radical act of salvation in Jesus Christ, cutting right to the heart of the human condition (Jer 31:31-33; Heb 8).

So, when Jesus begins his earthly ministry proclaiming, "Repent, for the kingdom of heaven has come near" (Matt 3:17), this is indeed good news! Jesus came to proclaim, enact and embody the in-breaking reality of God's eternal kingdom, for Israel and the world. The indications that this kingdom is nothing like those of this world are clear from start to finish. From the lowly manger to the degradation of the cross, Jesus is a king like no other for a kingdom like no other.

Quoting from Isaiah 61:1-2, Jesus sets out the "manifesto" for his kingdom work:

> [18] "The Spirit of the Lord is on me,
>   because he has anointed me
>   to proclaim good news to the poor.
> He has sent me to proclaim freedom for the prisoners
>   and recovery of sight for the blind,
> to set the oppressed free,
> [19] to proclaim the year of the Lord's favor." (Luke 4:18-19)

In his Sermon on the Mount, we begin to learn what characterizes this kingdom, who its citizens will be, and the blessings they will receive:

> ³ "Blessed are the poor in spirit,
>> for theirs is the kingdom of heaven.
> ⁴ Blessed are those who mourn,
>> for they will be comforted.
> ⁵ Blessed are the meek,
>> for they will inherit the earth.
> ⁶ Blessed are those who hunger and thirst for righteousness,
>> for they will be filled.
> ⁷ Blessed are the merciful,
>> for they will be shown mercy.
> ⁸ Blessed are the pure in heart,
>> for they will see God.
> ⁹ Blessed are the peacemakers,
>> for they will be called children of God.
> ¹⁰ Blessed are those who are persecuted because of righteousness,
>> for theirs is the kingdom of heaven.
> ¹¹ Blessed are you when people insult you, persecute you
> and falsely say all kinds of evil against you because of me.
> (Matt 5:3-11)

Jesus proclaims the advancement of the kingdom of heaven, for it is as assured as the mighty growth of a tiny mustard seed (Matt 4:30-32), as precious as "a pearl of great price" (Matt 13:46 KJV) and will be as rightfully and effectively claimed by its Lord as any earthly property (Matt 21:33-41). Jesus teaches his disciples to pray, "Your kingdom come, Your will be done" (Matt 6: 10), enacts his kingdom power in healings and exorcisms, and announces a new kingdom treaty sealed with his own blood (Luke 22:20; Heb 12:24).

If there were any remaining doubt as to the radical, upside-down nature of this kingdom, the means to Jesus' final victory over sin and death puts paid to this. Torture, degradation and a long and painful death are the inevitable consequences of his rejection of any form of coercive power. Yet, in their depiction of the trial and crucifixion of Jesus, the Gospel writers are clear that the reality of Jesus' true kingship as David's heir and God's beloved son cannot be suppressed. The leaders, both Jewish and Roman, may intend their words and actions to make a mockery of Christ the King but instead they play into the hands of God's revelation of his radical kingdom:

> Pilate also had an inscription written and put on the cross. It read, "Jesus of Nazareth, the King of the Jews." Many of the Jews read this inscription, because the place where Jesus was crucified was near the city; and it was written in Hebrew, in Latin, and in Greek. Then the chief priests of the Jews said to Pilate, "Do not write, 'The King of the Jews,' but, 'This man said, I am King of the Jews.'" Pilate answered, "What I have written I have written." (John 19:19-22)

The vindication of Jesus' kingship through his resurrection and ascension completes the picture: Christ has won the decisive victory over sin and death and is now exalted, reigning with complete authority, "at the right hand of God" (Matt 26:64; Heb 12:2; 1 Pet 3:22), until all his enemies are defeated and destroyed (1 Cor 15: 24-26).

Finally, for now, our focus turns to the fulfilment of the kingdom which is yet to come. God *is* king, Christ *has* inaugurated the kingdom, he *does* reign, and he *will* come again in glory as judge and redeemer to perfect the kingdom. And yet we are those, poised between Jesus' ascension and return, who are called to play our part in this "now and not yet" time. We cannot "bring" or "build" the kingdom because this prerogative and power belongs to God alone, and yet, by every means at our disposal, *we are called to live kingdom shaped lives in kingdom shaped churches*, all the while longing for a new heaven and a new earth in which all God's people will live, in God's place, under God's perfect rule (Rev 21:1-4). We'll come back to the Church's role in this throughout our remaining chapters, but this is the big picture of what we're all about.

Practical Theology and the Local Church

This vision of the kingdom is at the heart of what we want to help you achieve in leading vital churches. But how does it translate into practice in your local church? This is the very kind of question that Practical Theology seeks to answer. Bonnie Miller-McLemore advocates that one distinctive of Practical Theology is its tangible, local, concrete and embodied nature.[6] This theology isn't done in abstraction or disconnection from a local context but rather right in the midst of life's complexity.

This groundedness in real life means that this book doesn't contain answers. Instead, our aim is to provide you, a local church leadership, with processes and resources to work out what your church, in its tangible, local, concrete and embodied form of the kingdom, should and could be doing. This is why it is useful to think of Practical Theology as a verb rather than a noun. It is not so much a *thing* to possess, as something you *do*. It is not a fixed body of knowledge or answers, but a process, and a way of thinking, that is active and dynamic.

Practical Theology has another distinctive feature. Not only does it emerge from theological engagement with tangible, local, concrete and embodied life, it also engages with human wisdom. It recognises that God has blessed humanity with inquisitiveness and intelligence and that we can use these things in the service of his Church. This is part of the common grace we enjoy from the hand of God. Practical Theology is willing to utilise human endeavours like sociology, psychology and anthropology to better understand the local church and the world in which it exists. God's kingdom co-opts what is good and true for its own purposes.

The confidence to use these forms of "science" (knowledge of the world around us) in the service of the Church comes from the precedent of the wisdom literature of the Old Testament. In a sense, Solomon and his colleagues were Practical Theologians – they brought their theology into conversation with what they observed in the world to develop advice on how to live wisely. Theology, based on Scripture and worked out across the centuries of church history, will always take precedence over human knowledge but, as we hope you'll discover, the wisdom that stems from this knowledge can often bring helpful perspectives to theology.

The Nine "Vital" Dimensions of Church Life

This book has nine chapters, each chapter focusing on one feature of local church life which contributes to church health or vitality in service of the kingdom of God. These dimensions are not chosen on a whim, but on the basis of over a dozen separate research projects into church health which have been meta-analysed[7] by the Australian National Church Life Survey team, to identify those features of church life which consistently emerge as important for church vitality and health.[8] According to this meta-analysis, the most commonly identified features of church life that contribute to vitality are community, outward focus, leadership, spirituality, worship, discipleship, prayer, vision, caring for the young and giving.[9] Foster these, so the research says, and your church is more likely to be vital and flourishing. The unique contribution this book offers is to bring these sociological findings into conversation with theology and church history in order to develop best practice for local churches. In doing so we hope to help you avoid both blind praxis and blind theology.

However, knowing the theology, history and social science relating to church vitality is not the end of the process. In fact, it is just the beginning. It's one thing to understand community, for example, from both a theological and scientific perspective, but another thing to then identify what we will call "orthopraxis" for your particular church.[10] Orthopraxis, or literally "straight practice," is what emerges when having done the work of bringing theology and wisdom into conversation we ask, "In light of these resources, how should we live and what should we do?" Specifically in this book, we focus on enabling you to discern how your church should live and function in relation to each of the dimensions of church vitality.

But wait there's more... Even orthopraxis is not the end of the process. The final step in the practical theological exercise is the development of action steps to *achieve* orthopraxis in your unique context. What are you *going to do* to see this process through in order to help your church play its part in God's kingdom? It's not about "the way we have always done things around here" (traditionalism) or "what worked for the church down the road" (pragmatism) but discerning and acting on God's particular plan for you to be a kingdom-shaped church.

A Process of Practical Theology

There are many models of Practical Theology. We are going to use one that is particularly suited for the task we are encouraging you to undertake in your local church. For each of the nine vitality-giving features of local churches — kingdom aligned vision, strong community, outward focus, empowering leadership, vibrant faith, inspiring worship, intentional discipleship, caring for the young, and generous giving — we will be following the same process outlined below.

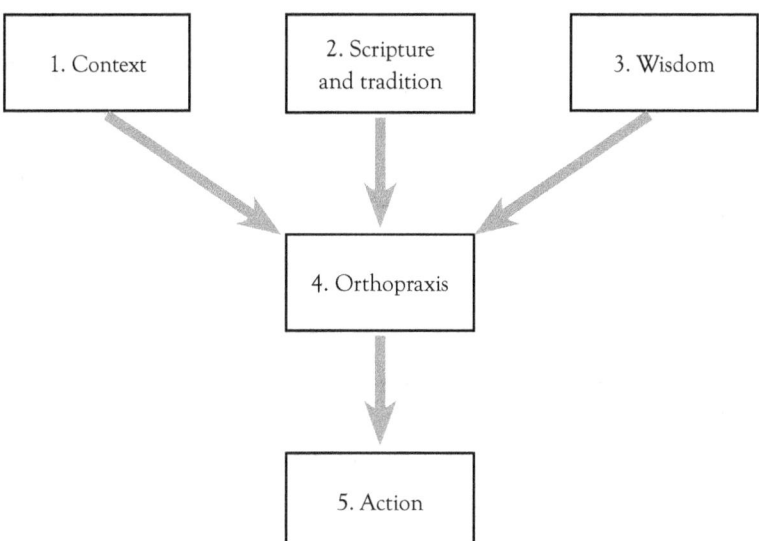

Step 1: Context

The first step in your exercise in Practical Theology, which you will repeat for each vital feature, is to accurately understand and describe a particular dimension in your local church. It's always tempting to rush this part of the process, but we've learnt from our own experience that you might well be surprised by what you learn if you take the time to openly and attentively observe what's going on in your church. Richard Osmer describes this step as "priestly listening,"[11] and you'll be aiming for what sociologists call a "thick" description of what each feature looks like in your context.[12] Your church already has the nine vital features identified by the research, to at least some extent, in an entirely unique way. Using the questions provided in each chapter we will help you to understand and describe *what* you do, and perhaps more importantly, *why* you do the things you do.[13] This step is a crucial starting point.

Step 2: Scripture and tradition

Few Christians would disagree with the idea that the Bible, and theology based on it, should strongly influence the way that churches operate. Indeed, there is a whole discipline devoted to this topic – ecclesiology. This technical term is actually two Greek words put together. The "eccles" part comes from the Greek word used to describe an assembly of people called out for a certain purpose. The New Testament frequently uses this term to describe the group of people we now refer to as a church. The "ology" part of the word comes from the Greek word for science. So, ecclesiology is, literally, the theological science of church. For each of the nine features of church life that foster church vitality, we will be presenting you with some scripturally informed, kingdom focused ecclesiology on which to base your Practical Theology.

However, we are not the first people to have ever sought to apply Scripture to the operation of the Church. In fact, people have been trying to do so for over 2000 years! And so, in a spirit of humility we will also be bringing you examples of the way in which the men and women who have gone before us have worked out their theology and sought to foster each of the nine features of church vitality down through the centuries. Their context was probably different to yours, and they will often stand in a different tradition to yours, but their experiences will widen your perspective, enable you to identify your blind-spots and guide you towards a sense of what you should be aiming for. In contrast to the traditionalism which blindly follows what has been done in the past, our inclusion of tradition represents an appreciation for the lessons God has, sometimes repeatedly, taught the Church over the centuries, and will enrich and enliven our grasp on ecclesiology.

Step 3: Wisdom

In the third step we will bring some wisdom to bear on the development of each of the nine features of church vitality. This wisdom will draw on three sources:

- Social Science — psychology, sociology and anthropology
- Congregational studies — scientific investigations into church life
- Best Practice — insights that can be gained from exemplary cases

These sources of wisdom should never take precedence over Scripture. However, they can give fresh insights on theology and inform its application in particular contexts. Step two will often provide churches with a "what" to do in general theoretical terms. Step three, wisdom, will often provide the "how" to do it in more practical and specific terms. Provided it does not contradict our scripturally based theology, human wisdom can be an extremely useful resource and provide ideas for ways ahead.

Step 4: Orthopraxis

By thoughtfully and prayerfully considering context, theology and wisdom, a local church leadership can develop orthopraxis for their particular church. Each local church has its own particular strengths and weaknesses and a particular context in which it is called to operate. What has worked in another context isn't guaranteed to work in yours. As a local church leadership you are uniquely positioned, and commissioned by God, to provide humble and prayerful leadership to your church community. Our hope, and motivation for writing this book is that you will lead your church, not purely on the basis of "the way we have always done things around here," or "the way that that successful church down the road does it," but on the basis of thoughtfully and prayerfully developing orthopraxis through your practical theological activity. In this section of each chapter, we'll be highlighting some of the principles which emerge from theology and wisdom, but you will need to explore these and decide if and how they work for you.

Step 5: Action

Pragmatically minded people really love the book of James, especially 1:22: "Do not merely listen to the word, and so deceive yourselves. Do what it says." All of us would agree that simply *knowing* what and how to do what is right is not enough. Grasping a vision of the kingdom, and even knowing how we might play our part, won't suffice. We need to *do* it.

However, it is very easy to be overwhelmed when we see too many things that we need to do. From our experience for most churches five deliberate, meaningful, action steps will be about as many as you can handle in a given year. There is no point identifying 20 action steps if you simply don't have the capacity to implement them. And, as always, change will take careful and prayerful planning. You'll need to consider how you bring your congregation on this journey and who will be impacted by these plans. Churches have complex problems and there are no "silver bullets" that will solve all your church's issues and enable it to become instantly vital. Instead, there are the numerous small interventions that will gradually edify your local church so that it more fully resembles the kingdom vision that God has for it.

And so, in the final step of your practical theological exercise, we will be asking you to identify a small number of steps you can take to foster the feature of church vitality addressed in each chapter. Your priorities in this process will be shaped according to what emerges for your church from our first chapter on "Kingdom Aligned Vision." Of course, we hope your commitment to orthopraxis will last for more than one year. The work of the kingdom will go on until Jesus' return! So, we are hoping that the practical theological exercise you complete as you work your way through this book will become a pattern for you. We pray that every year you will decide together what God is leading you to focus on and that you'll continue to flourish as a local church.

Conclusion

We've now introduced you to both the why and how of church vitality. The "why" is God and the gospel of his kingdom (what could be better than that!) and the "how" is the process of Practical Theology. We know all too well the sheer hard work that goes into leading a local church and the effort it takes to persevere in the face of what can seem like insurmountable difficulties or overwhelming options. We want to encourage you! Our aim is to help you find good and godly ways forward that enable you to overcome the obstacles and pick your way through the many possibilities for local church ministry. So, let's begin!

Chapter Endnotes

1. David Andrew Smith, *"Practical Theological Ecclesiology: Grounding, Integrating, Aligning and Improving Ecclesial Theory and Praxis in the Christian Brethren Community in Australia"* (University of South Africa, 2016), 13.

2. James Woodward, Stephen Pattison, and John Patton, *The Blackwell Reader in Pastoral and Practical Theology* (Oxford: Blackwell, 2000), 7.

3. Nicholas Perrin, *The Kingdom of God: A Biblical Theology*, ed. Jonathan Lunde, (Grand Rapids: Zondervan Academic, 2019), 40–41.

4. Graeme Goldsworthy, 'Gospel and Kingdom', in *The Goldsworthy Trilogy:* (Milton Keynes; Brentwood: Paternoster, 2006), 53.

5. Walter Brueggemann, *Theology of the Old Testament: Testimony, Dispute, Advocacy* (Minneapolis: Fortress Press, 1997), 431.

6. Bonnie J. Miller-McLemore, "Introduction," in *The Wiley-Blackwell Companion to Practical Theology*, ed. Bonnie J. Miller-McLemore (Chichester: Wiley-Blackwell, 2012), 7.

7. A meta-analysis is an activity that combines and synthesises a range of research related to the same topic in order to develop a model that incorporates all of the research.

8. Ruth Powell, Miriam Pepper, Nicole Ward, Sam Sterland and Kathy Jacka, *"Models of Church Vitality: A Literature Review,"* NCLS Occasional Paper 39 (2019).

9. Though drawing heavily on the meta-analysis in this book we will be combining the two vital features identified as "spirituality" and

"prayer," into one chapter we will call "Vibrant Faith." You will see why when we get to that chapter and in Appendix 2.

10 Just as orthodoxy is used to describe right-thinking, orthopraxis is right-action. In the same way that orthodoxy is informed by Scripture and tradition, so is orthopraxis.

11 Richard R. Osmer, *Practical Theology: An Introduction* (Grand Rapids: Eerdmans, 2008), 34.

12 Sociologists distinguish between thin description (for example a rapid closing and opening of an eyelid) and thick description (a wink) of the same event or situation.

13 You'll find supplementary questions for each section to help you dig deeper in the Appendix.

Chapter 1
Kingdom Aligned Vision

Introduction

Love them or loathe them, GPS navigational systems are with us to stay. We all have our horror stories about being led astray into dead ends or seemingly endless loops but, if we're honest, they make our lives so much easier. There is, of course, one vital piece of information we're going to need for a successful journey: our destination. Without an address, or at least the name of a suburb, we're going nowhere! And there's something else we need to consider: our destination will also inform the mode of transport we're going to use to get there. Our local cafe? We search for a walking or cycle route. A regional shopping centre? That's going to probably be a car journey. Heading overseas? Sea or air will be the way to go.

A clear sense of where we're heading as local churches is just as vital. As we'll explore below, in one sense we're all heading in the same direction - the kingdom of God in all its fullness when Christ returns. Yet this vision is so profound and all-encompassing that, in his mercy, God often calls us as individuals and churches to focus on specific aspects of his kingdom work. It's not that we can then forget about every other form of kingdom life, but God gives us a focused role to play which fits with his wider vision for the gospel of his kingdom. This focused sense of *what* God is calling our church to be is what we mean by "kingdom aligned vision." Then, as we saw with our navigational system, our kingdom destination must also shape *how* we plan to get there. We'll be unpacking what this means across many areas of church life in the following chapters, but we can be certain that kingdom purposes cannot be achieved by methods which fail to embody kingdom values.

It's just as well to get this theological starting point related to vision straight because we might otherwise get swallowed up by the sheer volume of material on the topic and, in particular, the art and science of creating vision statements. The Google books Ngram viewer,[1] which analyses the frequency of words and phrases in the vast Google books digital library, shows that, although the word "vision" has appeared in literature fairly consistently for the last 200 years, its usage has exploded since 1980. We recognise that your response to the word "vision" may well be a sense of weariness and futility. Too many vision statements have taken up too much time for far too little return. It is our observation that these vision statements are often poorly conceived, of little value and rarely operationalised. Churches often invest huge amounts of effort in developing and publicising their vision statements for a time but, apart from appearing on the church bulletin and website and being quoted by pastors, their existence or nonexistence makes little difference to the life of the church.

However, in this chapter we hope to lay a good theological foundation for the importance of developing a kingdom aligned vision for your church, and to provide some wisdom for how to go about doing something with it. We firmly believe that fixing our eyes on the gospel of the kingdom and engaging in godly and wise methods by which to discern and pursue our calling, will deeply refresh you and your church community, bringing new life and vitality to your labours. As frustrating as you may have found the question of vision in the past, our prayer is that by the end of this chapter you will be convinced of its value and be able to develop and use your kingdom aligned vision to energise your church.

Upfront, it will be helpful to give some definitions of terms at this point. The language around vision can be quite confusing. Whether you choose to use these terms or not, they provide a useful framework as you consider the various aspects of your kingdom aligned vision:

- Vision: A God-given picture of a better, kingdom-aligned future
- Core values: Principles that guide a person's or church's conduct
- Mission: What a church does, or should be doing, to fulfil this vision
- Goals: Landmarks along the way to the fulfilment of a vision
- Strategies: The "how-tos" of achieving goals

Step 1: Context

To begin, we recognise that even if your church does not have a "vision statement" it might still have a strong sense of vision. We also recognise that your church may already have a vision statement with an associated mission statement, core values and goals. If either case applies to you, please still use the processes set out in this chapter to reflect on your church's vision: your work here will form an important basis for the work in our remaining chapters. If you don't yet have a vision statement, or it is due for revision, we hope you'll take this opportunity to explore how developing one might be an important starting point for growing your church's vitality.

Your context may also include your church's membership of, or affiliation with, a denomination, network or movement. You may want or need to consider how the vision statement and other associated documents endorsed by this body, might impact the development of your church's particular vision statement.

The National Church Life Survey has identified that one of the core qualities related to vitality is "A Clear and Owned Vision." These are particularly useful adjectives to describe a helpful church vision. "Clear," usually reflects simple and concise language. But it is important that it is also "owned" by the congregation. This implies that it is not just a nice sounding statement or theme, but something which has found a home in the heart of a church. So, if you have recently completed the NCLS your NCLS Church Life Profile it will be a great place for you to start as you explore your own particular context.

Please note that here and for every other set of questions in each chapter, there are supplementary questions provided in Appendices. The questions asked here will get you started, but if you'd like to delve deeper or feel that you need more ideas, please take some more time to explore.

Reflection questions 1.1

1) What do the NCLS results tell you about the clarity and ownership of vision in your church?

2) What are your reflections on your church vision statement (if you have one)?

3) How has this vision impacted the life and decision-making of your church in the last 12 months?

Step 2: Scripture and Tradition

In our Introduction we began to explore how the good news of God's kingdom is Scripture's constant theme. God *is* king, Christ *has* inaugurated the kingdom, he *does* reign, and he *will* come again in glory as judge and redeemer to perfect the kingdom. Yet, as we also pointed out there, we are those poised between Jesus' ascension and return, called to play our part in all that God is doing in this "now and not yet" time, living kingdom shaped lives in kingdom shaped churches.

For this vocation, we will need to grasp more of what the kingdom looks like and particularly focus our attention on what Scripture has to say about how we, as individuals and churches, are to align ourselves and participate with God in his kingdom work.

Although it is a constant theme, God's vision for his kingdom is conveyed in three particular ways.

God Reveals His Kingdom Vision through Jesus

The first and foremost way God conveys his vision for his kingdom on earth is through Jesus Christ: in his earthly ministry, his saving work on the cross, and his victorious resurrection and ascension. As we outlined in our introductory chapter, Jesus not only proclaims the gospel of the kingdom, he enacts and embodies the gospel of the kingdom. He leaves no aspect of salvation unaddressed: people are challenged to repent, and their sins forgiven; the hungry are fed; people are healed of their physical diseases and liberated from spiritual oppression; the religious who would stand between God and his people are rebuked; the marginalised are restored to community; the rich are exhorted to give... Insert your own favourite example of Jesus' kingdom life here! In word and deed, Jesus lives the kingdom. And then he dies for the kingdom. By no other means can God's kingdom purposes be fulfilled. So Jesus lays down his life so that his Father's sovereign justice and mercy can be served, and his people can enter into the fullness of salvation. Christ's victory, attested by his resurrection and ascension, is complete – his work is not half done but finished – and yet we are called to participate in the kingdom's ongoing labour by modelling our lives on his.

God Reveals His Kingdom Vision through the Church

The second way in which God reveals the nature of the kingdom is through the manner in which God's people are called live as its citizens. Jesus reinforces his modelling of a kingdom shaped life through his teaching on how his followers are to live their own kingdom shaped lives. Among many other things, they are to share the gospel like determined fishermen; pray like beloved children; lead like humble servants; steward resources like faithful workers; bear their cross like self-denying disciples; abide in him like growing branches; and love one another as he loves them:

> [34] I give you a new commandment, that you love one another. Just as I have loved you, you also should love one another. [35] By this everyone will know that you are my disciples, if you have love for one another." (John 13:34-35)

And in all this, like Jesus, his disciples themselves are now to "make disciples of all nations, baptizing them in the name of the Father and of the Son and of the Holy Spirit, and teaching them to obey everything that I have commanded you" (Matt 28:19-20).

In the remainder of the New Testament we learn that how the Church conducts itself in light of the kingdom is vital for its worship and witness. Its capacity to fulfill God's purposes depends on it, and all sorts of terms have been used to express this point: churches are meant to be a foretaste, an embassy, an outcrop or outpost of the kingdom. For N.T. Wright and Michael Bird:

> Our task is to be faithful to the empire of Jesus, the kingdom of God. We are to consider our churches as the advance guard of the kingdom, and to do our best to prepare for the day when what Revelation says has already happened will become fully and finally true, and the kingdoms of this world will become the kingdom of our God and his Messiah.[2]

Or, to put it another way, according to Stanley Grenz,

> The church... derives its purpose from God's activity in world. The Holy Spirit calls community of faith into being, in order

that it might proclaim Christ's kingdom message and live in the world as the company of those who acknowledge in the present the coming reign of God.³

God Reveals His Kingdom Vision through Glimpses of the Fulfilment

Like Jesus, our churches are called to proclaim, enact and embody the kingdom of God, for God's glory and the sake of his world, always with an eye to the "coming reign of God." And this brings us to the third way in which Scripture conveys God's vision for his kingdom to us. In his great mercy God sets before us a vivid picture of the fulfilment of his kingdom. From the Old Testament, we learn that a messianic figure will emerge, his rule impacting the whole of creation:

> ⁶ The wolf will live with the lamb,
> 　　the leopard will lie down with the goat,
> the calf and the lion and the yearling together;
> 　　and a little child will lead them.
> ⁷ The cow will feed with the bear,
> 　　their young will lie down together,
> 　　and the lion will eat straw like the ox.
> ⁸ The infant will play near the cobra's den,
> 　　the young child will put its hand into the viper's nest.
> ⁹ They will neither harm nor destroy
> 　　on all my holy mountain,
> for the earth will be filled with the knowledge of the LORD
> 　　as the waters cover the sea. (Isaiah 11:6-9)

And in the New Testament, we hear from John:

> Then I saw "a new heaven and a new earth," for the first heaven and the first earth had passed away, and there was no longer any sea. ² I saw the Holy City, the new Jerusalem, coming down out of heaven from God, prepared as a bride beautifully dressed for her husband. ³ And I heard a loud voice from the throne saying, "Look! God's dwelling place is now among the people, and he will dwell with them. They will be his people, and God himself

will be with them and be their God.⁴ 'He will wipe every tear from their eyes. There will be no more death'ᵘ or mourning or crying or pain, for the old order of things has passed away."
⁵ He who was seated on the throne said, "I am making everything new!" Then he said, "Write this down, for these words are trustworthy and true." (Rev 21:1-5)

For the Church, Christ's vision is equally astounding:

²⁵ Husbands, love your wives, just as Christ loved the church and gave himself up for her ²⁶ to make her holy, cleansing her by the washing with water through the word, ²⁷ and to present her to himself as a radiant church, without stain or wrinkle or any other blemish, but holy and blameless. (Eph 5:25-27. See also Rev 19:7; 21:2,9; 22:17)

Vision and Hope

So, by faith, we allow God's revealed vision of his kingdom to seize and align us with his kingdom purposes. What a challenge. But also what a source of hope. Christian hope is the experiential counterpart to the objective occurrence of Jesus' resurrection.⁴ If Jesus rose from the dead, anything is possible! The future kingdom exerts influence on the present through this hope it awakens in us. As Christians hope — as we long for God's kingdom — we anticipate its future consummation and bring it to expression in the present. And as our churches live with their eyes opened to the glorious hope based in the gospel of the kingdom, we see that it overflows to those around us:

May the God of hope fill you with all joy and peace as you trust in him, so that you may overflow with hope by the power of the Holy Spirit. (Rom 15:13)

A hope filled church will always have an expectation of a better future, and a vision statement is a description of what that better future looks like.

For example, Nehemiah had a vision of a restored Jerusalem. In his mind he could see the walls - all straight and high and strong. He could see the gates - of solid timber. In his mind's eye he could see the people, safe within the walls living and worshipping God. It was all there. And it was a God-given vision:

> I set out during the night with a few men. I had not told anyone what my God had put in my heart to do for Jerusalem. (Neh. 2:12)

God had "put something in his heart" – it was a burden. He had this mental picture of what could happen and he had this incredible desire to see it happen.

Church history provides great examples of faith communities who have been called to share the overflow of their hope through a focused vision for their kingdom work. Francis of Assisi began a movement of such communities who chose to live in solidarity with, and service to, the poor. Quakers were those who focused on the abolition of slavery and a rejection of all forms of coercion. And the early Methodists were passionate about the widespread preaching of the gospel and growth in personal holiness through discipleship in community. Each of these movements began with particular faith communities, and their distinctive visions have contributed to the *whole sense* of how we are to participate in the gospel of the kingdom.

The local church continues to be the hope of the world through its proclamation of the gospel and, in describing this kingdom future, the notion of "a vision" for our churches becomes clear. A hope filled church will always have an expectation of a better future and its vision, simply put, is a focused description of what this better future looks like.

Reflection Questions 1.2
1) What do you think is the most important insight for church vision emerging from this survey of Scripture and tradition?

2) What does this survey of Scripture and tradition tell you about your church's vision?

3) On a scale of 1 to 10, how hope-full is your church?

Step 3: Wisdom

Whilst only the Bible and theology steeped in Scripture's vision of God's kingdom can provide the "what" and "why" of the vision for our churches, we believe that wisdom of the sort derived from the social sciences and congregational studies, can assist us with the "how."

As we've seen, hope is intertwined with vision, and psychologist Charles Snyder has developed a widely-accepted model to add to our understanding.[5] Hope is not just an emotion (where emotion is understood to be a purely passive response to circumstances), but a positive motivational state. Hence, hope is something that can be fostered and nourished, and impacts the way we live, rather than something we passively experience.[6]

In his research Snyder approached community leaders, including politicians, clergy, educators, and business executives.[7] He asked all of them to name the most hopeful people they knew using whatever definitions of hope they wanted. Then, he interviewed as many people on their lists as he could. These hopeful people shared three things—goals, pathways, and agency. Although Snyder called these the "three components of hope," it may be more useful to think of them as the three conditions for hope to thrive.

Condition #1: Goals

The first condition for hope to thrive is to have something to hope for.

Condition #2: Pathways

The second condition for hope to thrive involves the ability to generate pathways. A pathway is a strategy or plan for achieving a goal. While pathways can be simple or complex, the important thing is that there is some sort of pathway towards the vision.

Condition #3: Agency

The final condition for hope to thrive involves nurturing personal agency. Agency refers to the sense that our actions contribute to achieving our goals — that what we do matters — and it is therefore vital to the motivation which enables us to stay engaged with our goals. Thoughts like, "It's hopeless," "There is no way we can succeed," or even, "It's not worth trying," kill motivation and agency. Language like, "Yes we can, through the power of God," build agency and motivation.

So, as leaders of churches determined to overflow with hope for the kingdom, we are looking for ways to give our churches sanctified goals, pathways and motivation through our kingdom aligned vision.

The Snowy Mountains Scheme provides a great secular example of the impact of the power of vision. This hydroelectricity and irrigation complex in south-east Australia, was constructed between 1949 and 1974 and consists of sixteen major dams; seven power stations; two pumping stations; and 225 kilometres of tunnels, pipelines and aqueducts. More than 100,000 people from over 30 countries travelled to the mountains to work on the Snowy, with up to 7,000 workers on the site at any one time. Seventy per cent of the workers were migrants from Germany, Greece, Ireland, Italy, Britain, Norway, Poland and the former Yugoslavia. Despite the post war tensions there was hardly any friction amongst the workers. Despite the many little things which could have divided the workers, an awareness of the big purpose brought them together.

The Snowy River Scheme demonstrates the power of a common, clear and well-owned vision to bring about great outcomes, including:

- Hope for the future
- Purpose for sacrifice
- Reason to risk
- Unity in diversity
- An ultimate standard
- Guidance in decision-making

As an example of a good church vision, you might want to take a look at the vision statement for Rise, the church planting initiative of Redeemer Presbyterian Church, New York.[8] And here are some other vision statements which might stimulate your imagination:

- A church whose people daily engage in the Word of God and regularly share the gospel on their frontlines.
- An intergenerational church where each is being discipled and where each disciples others.
- A church full of young families where parents are equipped and children are nurtured.
- A multi-congregational church touching the lives of (insert number) people per week.
- A Gospel-centered church that equips culture shaping Christians (Coral Ridge Presbyterian Church, Ft Lauderdale, FL).

- A church composed of small groups where discipleship, care and outreach occur.
- A church so engaged with its community that the community identifies it as "their church."
- A church that gathers people from across the city in order to equip and scatter them out to be the kingdom of God on their frontlines.
- A multicultural church where different ethnicities are celebrated in every part of church life.
- The Redeemer family of churches and ministries exist to help build a great city for all people through a movement of the gospel that brings personal conversion, community formation, social justice, and cultural renewal to New York City and, through it, the world (Redeemer Presbyterian Church (New York)).

Reflection Questions 1.3
1) If you have a church vision statement, how does it measure up according to the criteria discussed in this section?

2) Does your church vision need a tweak or do you need to start from scratch?

Step 4: Orthopraxy

Despite the recurrent theme of hope, especially in the New Testament, many churches feel hope-less. In the face of falling and ageing attendance, deterioration of buildings and the perception of an increasingly hostile environment, churches may despair and turn in on themselves as a way of finding comfort and protection. But the future is never hope-less for the Christian Church. The resurrection of Jesus means that the church always lives in hope, not only of the consummation of the kingdom of God, but of its work in this time as well. Such is the power of the resurrection that it "overflows" into the present life. It is in describing the better future, that is always possible because of the power of the resurrection, that the word and notion of "a vision" becomes relevant.

We believe there are a number of principles to be drawn from our exploration of vision from Scripture, theology and wisdom:

- Your local church vision should be aligned with God's vision for his kingdom. You need to be deeply familiar with this.
- Your church vision will be forward-looking and full of hope. While the Bible, and the Gospels in particular, teach us so much about God's kingdom from the past and into the present, the fullness of the kingdom lies in God's future – our future. Such a vision will be deeply inviting for those both within and beyond your church.
- Flowing on from this, your vision should be faith-based. First, the discernment processes involved in its development should be immersed in prayer. God's Spirit has a vital role to play in highlighting relevant Scripture and bringing hope to life. Second, your vision should be faith-based, not just because it has a clear spiritual and biblical basis, but in terms of going beyond "business as usual." In other words, it should be "supernatural" and so ambitious that it requires God to act in order for it to be fulfilled. It should not be so outrageous that it is discouraging, but it should be ambitious enough to move the church to prayer in order to see it fulfilled.
- Your vision statement must be clear and focused. While the "big picture" vision of God's kingdom must always play in the background, no church could possibly attempt to respond to every aspect of it with equal emphasis. There is a specific role which God has in mind for your church and identifying this with clear (simple and concise) language will encourage the whole congregation to engage with it. This specificity and clarity will then facilitate the identification of the values, mission, goals and strategies which are needed to support it. A good litmus test for this is that such a vision statement might well help you to decide what *not* to do. Not every form of ministry or mission, even when these are long-standing or particular favourites of certain members or leaders of the congregation, will "fit" with a clear and focused vision statement.
- And this vision should be owned by the whole church. Depending on your church leadership form and style, you may, or may not, be used to engaging the whole church community in discernment for vision and planning but, as our "Action" section

will show, everybody might well have something to contribute to this process. This will bear fruit in terms of the support of the whole church for this vision and commitment to its fulfilment. This in turn will give people a sense of agency – that there is something they are able to contribute to the effort required for this vision to become reality. Carrying through on this engagement will require intentionality and persistence. It is more than putting the vision statement on the website and your letterhead. Leaders need to talk about it, decisions need to be based upon it, and preachers need to indicate its relevance, as frequently as possible.

If these principles look like they might take an extended period to implement, that's because they will! The development of a vision for your church, and the various statements which will go with this, is not the work of a late-night meeting, or evening a weekend retreat. But it will be worth it.

Reflection Questions 1.4
1) What do you feel is the most important insight regarding kingdom aligned vision generated by this chapter?

2) Is there anything you are unsure of or disagree with?

3) What do you feel is the most important insight on kingdom aligned hope and vision *for your church* generated by this chapter?

Step 5: Action
As we read in Section 3, Snyder identifies three conditions for hope to guide our steps in developing a kingdom aligned vision for your church:
- Goals
- Pathways
- Agency

Develop a Vision Statement
God has already planted his vision for your church in your hearts. Just as Nehemiah could see the walls of Jerusalem long before they were

constructed (Neh 2:12), you have a vision of a better future for your church already in your heart. You might not have described it with words, but it is there. And this vision will be aligned with the aspects of the kingdom of God that you are most passionate about. For some churches your vision will be shaped by a desire to preach the Word and practice discipleship. For others it will be about a desire to see your church engaged with your community as a witness to the gospel. For others it will be a specific growth target. Whatever it is about the kingdom of God that resonates in your church, seek to put into words the church God is calling you to become.

This is a difficult task. And it becomes more difficult as more people are involved. It would be wonderful if everybody in a church simultaneously received the same vision from God. But that rarely happens. More often the leader or leaders discern a picture of a better future and begin to carefully share it with others. When other people hear that vision and respond with excitement and faith you can begin to share it with more people. If people do not "buy in" to the vision, you need to go back a step and take on board their feedback and seek to better discern God's vision for your church.[9]

Show the Pathways

The second action step is to develop a strategy to fulfil this vision. This involves making the vision the basis of the activities and decisions of the church. In fact, the best measure of the quality of a vision statement is, "Does our vision statement impact the life and decision-making of our church?" If your answer to that question is, "no" there are two possible reasons why. The first is that the vision statement is too vague or general and does not describe the better future of the church in sufficient detail. If that is the case, you need to refine it and make it more focused. The second reason a vision statement is not being implemented is that you do not have a strategic plan to fulfil it. Here is a simple strategic plan you may wish to begin with:

Vision:				
Goal	Strategies	Action Steps	By When	Done
1.	1.1	1.1.1		
		1.1.2		
		1.1.3		
	1.2	1.2.1		
		1.2.2		
		1.2.3		
	1.3	1.3.1		
		1.3.2		
		1.3.3		

This plan should be an ever-changing basis of discussion, task allocation and accountability for your leadership team. It may be that the first agenda item of each meeting is to go through the plan and update it in light of what has happened in the previous period.

Provide Agency

If the second condition for hope is providing structures, the third condition is providing the motivation. Any worthwhile vision will be difficult to achieve and have setbacks in its fulfilment. But the role of local church leaderships is to help people identify how they can play their part and to "rally the troops" by reminding them, "Through the power of God we can do this! Let's keep praying. Let's keep loving. Let's keep preaching. Don't give up!"

Conclusion

Each of the following chapters will explore other aspects of kingdom life which have been identified as having key roles to play in church vitality. This chapter may well have helped you prioritise which of these aspects you need to pursue most urgently, but we do hope that you'll consider all of them as together they provide the basis of a well-rounded approach to your church's kingdom life.

Many social commentators consider that the church in Australia is in a hopeless situation. An analysis of the statistics suggests they might be right. But don't be fooled by physical appearances. The resurrection of Jesus Christ, which is the cornerstone of the Christian faith, declares that nothing is impossible. Those who would seek to write off a struggling local church on the basis of physical appearance would be wise to hold off in their judgement. If God can raise Jesus from the dead, he can rejuvenate your church and empower it to do incredible things. God *is* king, Christ *has* established the kingdom, he *does* reign, and he *will* come again in glory as judge and redeemer to perfect his kingdom. So, never, never, never give up hope.

Chapter Endnotes

1 https://books.google.com/ngrams

2 N. T. Wright and Michael F. Bird, *The New Testament in Its World: An Introduction to the History, Literature, and Theology of the First Christians*, Illustrated edition (Grand Rapids: Zondervan Academic, 2019), 845.

3 Stanley J. Grenz, *Theology for the Community of God* (Grand Rapids: Broadman & Holman, 2000), 478.

4 Andrew J. Stobart, "*Towards a Model of Christian Hope: Developing Snyder's Hope Theory for Christian Ministry,*" Theology and Ministry 1 (2012): 10.

5 Charles R. Snyder, Kevin L. Rand, and David R. Sigmon, "*Hope Theory,*" in *The Handbook of Positive Psychology*, ed. Charles R. Snyder and Shane J. Lopez (Oxford: Oxford University Press, 2002), 258.

6 Andrew J. Stobart, (2012): 3.

7 David B. Feldman, "*The Three Conditions for Hope to Thrive,*" Psychology Today, https://www.psychologytoday.com/au/blog/supersurvivors/201906/the-three-conditions-hope-thrive.

8 https://rise.redeemer.com/rise-campaign-video

9 Deriving a focused, kingdom aligned vision statement which will bring benefits to your church may mean you need help from a denominational consultant. But it is not impossible for a local church leadership, like yourselves, to put into words a hope-filled vision of a better future which clearly describes your church's role in God's kingdom.

Chapter 2
Strong Community

Introduction

We hope that you've already begun to get the picture that our churches are called by God to be communities in which the kingdom of God comes to life here and now. It is impossible for them to be a foretaste, an embassy or an outcrop of the kingdom without the relationality which characterises kingdom life: "God's people, in God's place, under God's rule."[1] We are God's people, "the community that comes into existence as a result of [Christ's] kingly power."[2] As we gather in our churches "in the Spirit," we become his "dwelling place" (Eph 2:22). And as we live together according to the "royal law" of love (Jas 2:8), we submit ourselves to his rule. We seek to live kingdom shaped lives in kingdom shaped churches.

It is *this* community which is the hermeneutic of, or way to make sense of, the gospel of the kingdom:

> It is the community which has begun to taste (even only in foretaste) the reality of the Kingdom which alone can provide the hermeneutic of the message ... Without the hermeneutic of such a living community, the message of the Kingdom can only become an ideology and a programme; it will not be a gospel.[3]

The local church community is God's means, by the power of his Spirit, of manifesting the gospel to the world. When we fail as churches to live the gospel of the kingdom in our church communities, we misspeak the gospel of the kingdom. What does the world hear and see as it looks at our churches? Here is our challenge for your church community in this chapter: to become more like the kingdom of God for God's glory and the sake of his gospel for his world.

Given this strong connection between the gospel of the kingdom, the Church and community, it should be no surprise that almost every research project into church health and vitality has concluded that a strong sense of community is highly significant.[4] The terms associated with community in the empirical research into church vitality include authenticity,[5] hospitality,[6] relational intentionality,[7] loving relationships,[8] connections with each other,[9] a strong and growing sense of belonging, intentional and welcoming inclusion,[10] participating in the congregation and welcoming new people.[11]

Sociologists have also long been aware that a strong sense of community produces a whole range of benefits.[12] As we write this chapter much of the world is in "lockdown" in response to the spread of COVID-19 and social scientists are reminding us that loss of community raises the risk of isolation and loneliness and exerts pressure on our relationships and mental health.

But what do we actually mean by "community"? As Robert Wuthnow points out, when contemporary Westerners speak of finding community in a small group, they mean something quite different from what "community" has meant in the past.[13] Most contemporary Australians would think of community as something over which they have a great deal of control. They have chosen to join a particular group and they can withdraw relatively easily if it disappoints them. Their involvement with the group provides them with some emotional intimacy but generally does not provide, or require them to offer others, the physical or economic support that a community would traditionally provide. Further, emotional support is likely to be limited to encouragement rather than including correction or guidance. And although the relationships provided in a small group meeting may be helpful, this is not the same thing as sharing a home with extended family (parents, grandparents, aunts, uncles, cousins, in-laws) where the traditional understandings of community were grounded. This traditional, "intense" form of community that has existed throughout most of human history and still exists in many parts of the world, might well be a long way from the experience or expectations of the people in your church. We need to take this cultural context into account and yet still seek ways to engender kingdom shaped forms of community.

What might these forms of kingdom community look like, and how can they be developed? In this chapter we will help you define some orthopraxis with respect to community in your church and identify some action steps to enable it to flourish.

Step 1: Context

As with many of the dimensions of church vitality, your last National Church Life Survey (if you participated in it) is an excellent resource to inform your discussion of the sense of community which already exists among attenders. One of the nine core qualities the NCLS measures is "Sense of Belonging" which is helpful when seeking to measure the strength of community in your church. Please carefully consider the results for your church on this core quality.

A strong sense of community is not just marked by people shaking hands (or bumping elbows!) at church. It involves a deeper sense of commitment and partnership. And so, another way to measure the sense of community in your church would be to consider the percentage of the congregation who are involved in small groups or have a "significant" relationship with one or more people in the church. A "significant" relationship would be one that exists outside of the Sunday church gatherings and where important things are discussed. Although, as we have suggested above, small groups may, or may not, foster a strong sense of community, they are a reasonable way of estimating it. Go through your church roll and identify which members of the church are part of small groups or have significant relationships with others in the church and those who do not. This will give you a concrete way of measuring changes in the strength of community in your church.

You need to be aware that as people who have committed yourselves to leadership of a local congregation, you are likely to feel a very strong sense of community. You have probably been a part of the church for some time and have significant friendships and family connections in the church. But this may not be the experience of the majority of the people in your church. Be careful not to assume that *your* experience of community in your church is shared by everyone.

Reflection questions 2.1
1) What percentage of the church are involved in small groups?

2) What percentage of the church have "significant" relationships with other people in the church that function independently of organised church events?

3) What activities does your church have which foster strong community?

4) What other evidence do you have that your church has a strong sense of community? (Think back to some of the factors described in the Introduction to this chapter.)

Step 2: Scripture and Tradition

In the Old Testament, God elected Israel to be his people and, at least at their best, they knew themselves to be his "congregation" or "assembly," a community entirely defined by their relationship with him as their rescuer, redeemer and king.[14]

It was to this people that Jesus then came, proclaiming and enacting the gospel of the kingdom from within the community of his twelve disciples and the ever-widening circle of his followers. His intention was clearly to create a new form of covenant community to be God's kingdom people,[15] his flock and his family. This work was begun during his earthly ministry but, as he had always envisaged, his Church was birthed with the power of his resurrection through the Holy Spirit (Acts 2:1-4), and the preaching of the gospel (Acts 2:5-40). Those who heard the message repented and were baptized (Acts 2:41) — and began to be the Church.

As those living in our highly privatized and consumeristic society, we are often dazzled by what follows:

> [44]All who believed were together and had all things in common; [45] they would sell their possessions and goods and distribute the proceeds to all, as any had need (Acts 2:44-45).

But the key to this astounding behaviour lies in the much more "everyday" set of behaviours which knit this community together:

> [42] They devoted themselves to the apostles' teaching and to fellowship, to the breaking of bread and to prayer. [46] Every day they

continued to meet together in the temple courts. They broke bread in their homes and ate together with glad and sincere hearts, [47] praising God and enjoying the favor of all the people. (Acts 2:42, 46-47a)

It was as they sat together under the apostles' teaching that they learnt to trust that they were on the same kingdom page. It was as they shared hospitality and table fellowship together, that they began to understand one another's lives and their communion together in Christ. It was as they praised God together that they were reminded of his generosity to them in Christ which urged them to meet one another's' needs. And it was as they prayed together that they came to share their concerns and see one another through God's eyes. These actions were "everyday" and yet, empowered by the Spirit and Jesus' self-sacrificial model of love, profound and revolutionary. This was no ordinary human form of association.

As time passed, churches, both Jewish and gentile, sprang up in more geographically and culturally diverse contexts. Jesus' teaching had already prepared his followers to consider one another as family, and Paul highlighted their shared status as "sons,"[16] brothers and sisters under the fatherhood of God. In Greco-Roman culture sibling relationships were usually more important than sibling relationships in modern Western cultures.[17] However, for many new disciples, coming out of paganism resulted in the loss of these sibling relationships. Perhaps in response to this, Paul placed a heavy emphasis on Christians considering each other as brothers and sisters (1 Cor 1:11; 14:26) and highlighted the metaphor of the church as family:

> [10] Therefore, as we have opportunity, let us do good to all people, especially to those who belong to the family of believers. (Gal 6:10)

They were also Christ's body, in intimate relationship with one another in ways which completely disregarded the normal hierarchies of class, race and gender (1 Cor 12:12-31; Gal 3:28) and placed them in service to one another for the common good of the whole body with Christ as their head. As such "members one of another" (Rom 12:5), they were to exercise the many "one anothers" of the New Testament. They were to

- love one another (John 13:34-35; Rom 13:8; 1 Thess 4:9; 1 John 3-4)
- accept one another (Rom 14:1-15:7; James 2:1-9)
- belong to one another (Rom 12:4-5)
- teach and admonish one another (Rom 15:14; Eph 4:15; Col 1:28; 3:16; 1 Thess 5:14)
- confess sins to one another (Jas 5:13-16; 1 John 7-10)
- bear one another's burdens (Gal 6:1-2)
- encourage one another (1 Thess 4:18; 5:11; Heb 3:12-13; 10:25)
- spur one another on (Heb 10:24-25)
- be reconciled with one another (Matt 5:23-24; Eph 2:14-16)
- and forgive one another (Matt 18:32-33; Eph 4:32-5:2; Col 3:13; 1 Pet 4:8) [18]

All of which can be summed up in the Greek term, *koinonia*, which is translated "fellowship" and returns us to the picture Luke paints in Acts Chapter 2. As we've now seen, such fellowship meant so much more than sharing some food and laughter together. It was in fact the term used in the ancient world to describe the close and self-sacrificial partnership of the marital relationship.[19] The result of this deeper sense of *koinonia* then, and throughout church history, has been that "day by day the Lord added to their number those who were being saved" (Acts 2:47b).

In the following centuries, Rodney Stark describes how the dynamic of such *koinonia* revolutionised whole cities:

> Christianity served as a revitalization movement that arose in response to the misery, chaos, fear, and brutality of life in the urban Greco-Roman world... Christianity revitalized life in Greco-Roman cities by providing new norms and new kinds of social relationships able to cope with many urgent problems. To cities filled with the homeless and impoverished, Christianity offered charity as well as hope. To cities filled with newcomers and strangers, Christianity offered an immediate basis for attachment. To cities filled with orphans and widows, Christianity provided a new and expanded sense of family. To cities torn by violent ethnic strife, Christianity offered a new basis for social solidarity...[20]

Given the attractive power of the early Christian communities it might surprise us then to hear that the churches who so effectively shared the gospel of the kingdom exercised strong boundaries around their communities. In this they took their lead from Jesus himself who clearly recognised that not everyone would enter the kingdom of heaven (Matt 5:20; 7:21; 18:3; 19:23), and Paul who often drew distinctions between those who were "inside" and those who were "outside" (1 Cor 5:12, 13; Col 4:5; 1 Thess 4:12; 1 Tim 3:7). Paul Trebilco concludes:

> The outsider designations used by the early Christians raise the question of the relationship between group distinctiveness and attitudes to outsiders. Some of the designations used for outsiders can be seen as terms that make a strong distinction between "us" and "them" and so are strongly exclusionary terms. "Unbelievers", "outsiders", "the unrighteous", "sinners" and so on are terms that strongly exclude outsiders. They contribute strongly to a sense of group identity, and underline what distinguishes early Christians from others.[21]

It should be unsurprising, then, that one of the interesting features of the churches in the first few centuries of the Christian era was just how difficult they were to join! Membership of the Christian community was marked by baptism, and those who wished to be baptised were called *catechumeni*. According to the ancient document "(On The) Apostolic Tradition," before they could even apply to be baptised, "Catechumens will hear the word for three years. Yet if someone is earnest and perseveres well in the matter, it is not the time that is judged, but the conduct" (17:1-2).[22] In fact, Alan Kreider has proposed that it was this process of careful instruction in the faith and an expectation of a deeply Christian form of life — living kingdom shaped lives in kingdom shaped churches — which enabled the impact that Stark describes.[23]

Reflection questions 2.2

1) What do you think is the most important insight for church community emerging from this survey of Scripture and tradition?

2) What does this survey of Scripture and tradition tell you about *your* church community?

Step 3: Wisdom

As mentioned earlier, sociologists have a keen interest in community, or more specifically, people's sense of community, because of its wide-ranging emotional, social and health benefits. Sarason defined "sense of community" as the feeling that one is part of a readily available, supportive and dependable structure that is part of everyday life and not just available when disasters strike.[24]

The most widely accepted model of this sense of community is that of McMillan & Chavis.[25] They argue that a sense of belonging to, and identification with, a community involves a shared set of values, beliefs and rituals which create boundaries within which people feel safe to express feelings and needs. This, in turn, enables the development of a level of relational intimacy. While there are no guarantees, the frequency and meaningfulness of connecting with others in the community also helps. People who "belong" tend to believe they have some capacity to influence the decisions and practices of their community and, in turn, are open to the influence of their community on their own attitudes and behaviours. And there are shared stories about the past, the present and the future which provide common ground and a sense that "we're all in this together."

In 1995 Roy Baumeister and Mark Leary released a classic paper summarising the research on the "need to belong" as a fundamental human motivator. They conclude,

> The desire for interpersonal attachment may well be one of the most far-reaching and integrative constructs currently available to understand human nature.[26]

Little wonder then that sense of community is such an important factor not only in church life, but amongst humanity in general. Indeed, Bainbridge and Stark have demonstrated that the need to belong may be a more compelling factor in religious participation than belief — hence the phrase "belonging before believing."[27] Belief in certain doctrines may be a powerful motivator for Christian behaviour, but sociology would suggest that belonging to a community is also a highly significant factor.

Another important sociological insight on community is the distinction between community and *communitas*. Anthropologists identify *communitas* as characteristic of groups of people experiencing liminality (an experience of being "on the edge" or in a state of change) and rites of passage.[28] *Communitas* can be thought of as the intense sense of community one feels with a group of people in a challenging context. Ex-servicemen and women usually have a sense of *communitas* with their comrades in arms. Many Christians across the world and throughout history have experienced the sort of profound commitment to one another that could be described as *communitas* in the midst of religious persecution or collective sacrificial service for the sake of others. Such *communitas* adds a further dimension to a sense of belonging and community.

Reflection Questions 2.3
1) What does this survey of human wisdom tell you about church community?

2) What does this survey of human wisdom tell you about *your* church community?

Step 4: Orthopraxy

What principles can we draw together from our exploration of community in Scripture, tradition and wisdom?

We begin with the observation that in both kingdom and human terms, community is vital. There is no surprise here. God created us for himself and for the kingdom life which is inevitably relational. Church community is both divine and very human: empowered and united in Christ by the Holy Spirit *and* designed to meet one of our most fundamental human needs. It's by no means uncomplicated and often far from easy, but it is central to God's calling to live kingdom shaped lives in kingdom shaped churches and so demands our careful attention.

This form of community or *koinonia* is expressed in many "everyday" ways and yet remains profound and revolutionary. In both our larger church gatherings and small groups, worshiping God and studying his word together develops our shared values and beliefs. As we practice hospitality, sharing ordinary meals, we are humanly knit together, and as we share around the Lord's table, his Spirit reminds us of our communion in Christ. As we pray together, we share our concerns for ourselves and God's world, learning to see everything and everyone through God's eyes. And as we "one another" — being Christ's family and his body — we practice being the kingdom of God. Developing these foundational blocks of community, encouraging everyone to play their part, to give and receive, to bless and be blessed, is core church business.

Beyond this everyday-ness, we have seen that providing opportunities to develop more intense forms of *communitas* will build an even deeper sense of community. For Australian churches this might happen in the taxing context of a short-term mission trip or beach mission. It might be developed in the intensity of a church camp or retreat, or by working with a team on a community service or church building project. Promoting opportunities for as many church members as possible to engage in such activities will further enable them to develop a strong sense that they are indeed knitted together in community as God's people and Christ's body.

We have also seen that there is a creative tension between the boundaries which honour the nature of God's kingdom and ensure a sense of belonging, and the missional impulse to simply include everyone in every aspect of our church communities. The gospel is not that the kingdom has no boundaries but that, by grace through faith in Christ, everyone can and should experience warm and repeated invitations to cross them. This does not preclude but rather produces intentional practices for "belonging before believing." Like our children whom we "bear" with us in our relationship with God until they make their own confession of faith, we embrace those who are yet to enter the kingdom, knitting them into our community by every means appropriate to their as yet unbelieving status. Nevertheless, we need to celebrate our boundaries — in the initiatory rite of baptism, around the Lord's table, when discussing discipleship, commitment and membership issues — making sure that every time these are raised, there is a warm invitation to join the kingdom and a clear sense of how this can be done.

Reflection Questions 2.4
1) What do you feel is the most important insight on sense of community generated by this chapter?

2) What do you feel is the most important insight on sense of community *for your church* generated by this chapter?

3) What else could your church do to foster a stronger sense of community?

Step 5: Action

As we have highlighted, the practical theological process is not completed when orthodoxy is developed, but when it is implemented. So in this section of each chapter we ask you to identify action steps to ensure that good ideas become good practice. Here is a process which you might like to use or adapt for your context:

1) Gather together as a leadership and pray for the discernment of God's wisdom for your church with respect to its sense of community.

2) Share together your answers to Reflection Questions 2.4.

3) Individually, write down your answer to the following question: What should our church *do* to foster a stronger sense of community? You might come up with up to five suggestions. Try to make your suggestions as specific as possible. For example, rather than just saying "Foster a sense of *communitas* in the church," you could suggest something like "Ensure that we have a short-term mission trip every year," or, "Have a hospitality Sunday once a month where people in the church share meals together."

4) Go around the group and have each member suggest one action the church could take to foster a stronger sense of community. Write the suggestion on a whiteboard or similar media. If your suggestion has already been made put a tick next to it on the whiteboard and then share your next suggestion.

5) When everyone has shared all of their suggestions, each member in the group is allocated three votes. (You might like

to allocate each member three self-adhesive dots for this activity.) Each member can then use their votes. They can allocate all three votes to the same suggestion or utilise them across a number of suggestions.

6) Tally up the dots and you will have an indication of what, as a leadership team, might be a good action steps to take to develop sense of community in your church. Pray again and then decide which action steps you wish to take. Two or three is probably all that you can attempt at one time. Still, keep a record of your suggestions because you may be able to come back to them next year.

Conclusion

A strong sense of community is one of the fundamental dimensions of God's kingdom vision for the church and therefore, unsurprisingly, of church vitality. Even though you might feel a strong sense of community yourself, if you can foster a deeper sense of community across your church it will produce benefits in a whole range of areas, especially in your capacity to witness to the reality of the gospel of the kingdom. Remember, the way you live and labour together as God's people in your church, speaks, enacts and embodies this gospel. Our churches are called by God to be communities in which the kingdom of God comes to life here and now.

Chapter Endnotes

1   Graeme Goldsworthy, "*Gospel and Kingdom,*" in *The Goldsworthy Trilogy* (Milton Keynes; Brentwood: Paternoster, 2006), 53.

2   C. Réné Padilla, "The Mission of the Church in Light of the Kingdom of God," *Transformation* 1, no. 2 (1984): 17.

3   Lesslie Newbigin, *Sign of the Kingdom* (Grand Rapids: Eerdmans, 1980), 19.

4   Ruth Powell et al., "*Models of Church Vitality: A Literature Review,*" *NCLS Occasional Paper* 39 (2019): 13.

5   Scott B. McKee, "*The Relationship between Church Health and Church Growth in the Evangelical Presbyterian Church*" (Doctor of Ministry Dissertation. Asbury Theological Seminary, 2003).

6   Diana Butler Bass, *Christianity for the Rest of Us: How the Neighborhood Church Is Transforming the Faith* (New York: HarperOne, 2009).

7   Ed Stetzer and Thom S Rainer, *Transformational Church: Creating a New Scorecard for Congregations* (Nashville: B&H Publishing Group, 2010).

8   Christian A. Schwarz, *Natural Church Development: A Guide to Eight Essential Qualities of Healthy Churches* (7th *Updated and Revised Edition*) (St. Charles: Churchsmart Resources, 2006).

9   Linda Bobbitt, "*Measuring Congregational Vitality: Phase 2 Development of an Outcome Measurement Tool,*" *Review of Religious Research* 56, no. 3 (2014).

10 Ruth Powell et al., *Enriching Church Life*, 2nd ed. (Saint Mary's: Mirrabooka Press & NCLS Research, 2012).

11 Cynthia Woolever and Deborah Bruce, *Beyond the Ordinary: Ten Strengths of Us Congregations* (Louisville: Westminster John Knox Press, 2004).

12 Grace Pretty et al., "Psychological Sense of Community and Its Relevance to Well-Being and Everyday Life in Australia," The Australian Psychological Society, http://www.groups.psychology.org.au/Assets/Files/Community-Updated-Sept061.pdf.

13 Robert Wuthnow, *Sharing the Journey: Support Groups and America's New Quest for Community* (New York: Free Press, 1994), 16.

14 Paul D. Hanson, *The People Called: The Growth of Community in the Bible* (San Francisco: Harper & Row, 2001), 24-26.

15 N. T. Wright, *Jesus and the Victory of God*, Christian Origins and the Question of God; (London: SPCK, 1996), 246.

16 This is one of those times when it is helpful to maintain the gendered nature of biblical language. "Sonship" was a status of great privilege in first century Palestine, and our sonship is derived from that of Jesus himself. One of the wonders of the Christian faith is that, from the outset, this term was applied to all God's children, both male and female, in Christ. See, for example, Brian S. Rosner, *Known by God: A Biblical Theology of Personal Identity*, ed. Jonathan Lunde (Grand Rapids: Zondervan, 2017), 157.

17 Reider Aasgaard, "Brothers and Sisters in the Faith," in *The Formation of the Early Church*, ed. Jostein Adna (Tubingen: Mohr Siebeck, 2005), 288.

18 Thomas Jones and Steve Brown, *One Another: Transformational Relationships in the Body of Christ* (Spring Hill Discipleship Publications International, 2008), 8-11.

19 William F. Arndt, Frederick W. Danker, and Walter Bauer, *A Greek-English Lexicon of the New Testament and Other Early*

Christian Literature, 3rd ed. (Chicago: University of Chicago Press, 2000), 552.

20 Rodney Stark, *The Rise of Christianity* (Princeton University Press, 1996), 161.

21 Paul Trebilco, "Outsider Designations in the New Testament," https://www.bibleinterp.com/PDFs/TrebilcoPDF.pdf (2018); Paul Raymond Trebilco, *Outsider Designations and Boundary Construction in the New Testament: Early Christian Communities and the Formation of Group Identity* (Cambridge: Cambridge University Press, 2017).

22 Attributed to Hippolytus of Rome around, around 235 CE.

23 Alan Kreider, *The Patient Ferment of the Early Church: The Improbable Rise of Christianity in the Roman Empire* (Grand Rapids: Baker Academic, 2016), 134.

24 Seymour Bernard Sarason, *The Psychological Sense of Community: Prospects for a Community Psychology* (San Francisco: Jossey-Bass, 1974).

25 Pretty et al., 6.

26 Roy Baumeister and Mark Leary, "*The Need to Belong: Desire for Interpersonal Attachments as a Fundamental Human Motivation,*" Psychological Bulletin, 117 (1995): 522.

27 Rodney Stark and William Sims Bainbridge, *The Future of Religion: Secularization, Revival, and Cult Formation* (Berkley: University of California Press, 1985), 316-23.

28 Edith Turner, *Communitas: The Anthropology of Collective Joy* (Springer, 2012).

Chapter 3
Outward Focus

Introduction

God's kingdom vision is for the whole of his world to recognise his kingship, to repent and believe, and enter into the blessings of his kingdom. God *is* king, Christ *has* inaugurated the kingdom, he *does* reign, and he *will* come again in glory as judge and redeemer to perfect the kingdom. A time will come when every knee *will* bow and every tongue confess "that Jesus Christ is Lord, to the glory of God the Father" (Phil 2:9-11). Our work as churches in this "now and not yet time" is to play our part in ensuring that this kingdom summons is communicated by every possible means to the whole of God's world. To be aligned with this vision, local churches need to be focused beyond themselves on those parts of the world where God's kingdom is not yet recognised. But as C.S. Lewis pointed out:

> There exists in every church something that sooner or later works against the very purpose for which it came into existence. So, we must strive very hard, by the grace of God, to keep the church focused on the mission that Christ originally gave to it.[1]

It is amazing how the words of C.S. Lewis remain so relevant to the 21st century Australian Church!

Another feature of church vitality that the empirical research identifies is the need for churches to be, what we will call, outwardly focused. The terms related to this dimension used by empirical researchers include intentional evangelism,[2] missionary mentality,[3] need-oriented evangelism,[4] testimony, justice,[5] connections with the world,[6] practical and diverse service, willing and effective faith sharing,[7] focusing on the community and sharing faith.[8] Most of us would warmly affirm the importance of outward focus as described by these terms. However, as Lewis points out, churches face a constant battle to resist the temptation to become inwardly focused, rather than focused on those beyond their church communities.

There are two dimensions to outward focus. The first one might be called awareness. This may be measured by how often the events of the world are mentioned in our various church gatherings and communications. For example, as we write there are race protests going on across the world in the wake of the death of George Floyd and the #blacklivesmatter movement. Some churches would be seeking to address this issue. Others would consider that addressing such issues is not "core business" for the church and seek to avoid them. This may be fine, but it does reflect, in one sense, a more inward focus. Our concern for, and ongoing solidarity with the broken world, like that of Christ with fallen humanity, positions us to intercede and labour for it — in word and deed — out of humility and compassion.[9]

A second dimension to outward focus for churches, is the more specific area of engaging those outside the church with the gospel of the kingdom. Generally, when church folk talk about being outwardly focused, they are referring to how actively their church is involved in evangelism. This feature of church life will be the major focus of this chapter.

Step 1: Context

The NCLS model of church vitality has two core qualities that relate to outward focus. They are "Practical and Diverse Service," and "Willing and Effective Faith Sharing." Please have a look at your most recent NCLS survey results to make an objective assessment of how outwardly focused your church is. It might also be worth reflecting upon the percentage of "Newcomers" (people who have joined the church in the previous five years but previously had not been attending anywhere) as a measure of the effectiveness of the church's outward focus.

The other thing to consider is the ministries of the church which are outwardly focused. Use the table like the one below to clarify the focus of all of your church's ministries.

Ministry/Activity	Mainly focused on those inside the church	Focused on both those inside the church and outside the church	Mainly focused on those outside the church
Worship services	✓		
Carols service		✓	
Alpha courses			✓

Reflection Questions 3.1
1) What would it look like if our church was outwardly focused? Are we?

2) What does our NCLS survey reveal about our church's outward focus?

3) What other evidence is there that our church is outwardly focused?

Step Two: Scripture and Tradition

The outward focus of God's people can be traced to early on in the outworking of God's redemptive plan:

> The LORD had said to Abram, "Go from your country, your people and your father's household to the land I will show you.
>
> ² "I will make you into a great nation,
>   and I will bless you;
> I will make your name great,
>   and you will be a blessing.
> ³ I will bless those who bless you,
>   and whoever curses you I will curse;
> and all peoples on earth
>   will be blessed through you. (Gen 12:1-3)

Abraham and his family were blessed by God in order that they may be a blessing to all the peoples on earth. This is reiterated by Isaiah when God declares:

> I will also make you a light for the Gentiles,
> that my salvation may reach to the ends of the earth. (Isa 49:6)

The metaphor of light implies that the "brightness" of Israel would shine out to the nations around them and attract them to salvation. As pointed out by Christopher Wright, God's blessing of an individual, family, or nation tends to "overflow" to those around them. It is "self-replicating."

> Those who are blessed are called to be a blessing beyond themselves — and this is one feature that makes it [the blessing of Abraham] so profoundly missional. For if we see ourselves (as we should, according to Paul in Galatians) as those who have entered into the blessing of Abraham through faith in Christ, then the Abrahamic commission becomes ours also — "be a blessing."[10]

The blessings bestowed on Israel were not just for their own sake, but a way of convincing the nations to seek Yahweh and his kingdom for themselves. Even in exile the people of Israel were to be a blessing (Jer 29:7), and Daniel demonstrates how to draw people (like Nebuchadnezzar) into relationship with God through witnessing the blessing Daniel received because of his obedience to God.

However, while Daniel is a powerful example of God working through individuals, God's redemptive plan has generally been built around the communities, or assemblies, of his chosen people who are mobilised to be light to the world. Jesus takes Israel's missional mandate to be a corporate light to the nations and applies it to his disciples by the use of the plural "you" in Matthew 5:14-15:

> [14] "You are the light of the world. A town built on a hill cannot be hidden. [15] Neither do people light a lamp and put it under a bowl. Instead they put it on its stand, and it gives light to everyone in the house."

Indeed, according to John 13:35 (and as we explored in Chapter 2), it is the powerful relationships that exist between disciples that will be their primary identifier to non-believers:

> "By this everyone will know that you are my disciples, if you love one another."

Hence, as we explored in the previous chapter, the proclamation of the gospel shines outwards through the strong sense of community that exists amongst those who seek to live kingdom shaped lives in kingdom shaped churches. As Gibbs and Bolger point out, "A community committed to the gospel of the reign of God provides a most convincing apologetic of the gospel."[11] An unchurched person will normally struggle to accept the truths of Christianity as an outside observer. They need to first experience the embodied truth of kingdom community and the blessing that comes with it by observing the relationships that exist between believers and experiencing that love for themselves. They often belong before they believe, but by God's grace and with our intentional labours, they *do* come to believe.

However, the metaphor of the church as a light attracting others to the kingdom should not lead to passivity. The outward focus of the Church is not only suggested by the metaphor of it being light, but by the very nature of the one who calls it. One of the amazing dimensions of the Trinity revealed in the Scriptures is its sending nature. After the resurrection Jesus appears to his disciples and says in John 20:

> [21] "Peace be with you! As the Father has sent me, I am sending you."[22] And with that he breathed on them and said, "Receive the Holy Spirit."

As the Father sends the Son on a mission to inaugurate his kingdom, so the Son sends the Church to continue his mission through the powerful agent of the Holy Spirit. "Christ has been enthroned as King and his sovereignty extends over the totality of Creation. As such he commissions his disciples to make disciples of all nations"[12]:

> [19] "Therefore go and make disciples of all nations, baptizing them in the name of the Father and of the Son and of the Holy Spirit,

²⁰ and teaching them to obey everything I have commanded you. And surely I am with you always, to the very end of the age." (Matt 28: 19-20)

Although the main verb of this verse has traditionally been translated as "go" there is a good case for translating it in the participle form, "going" or "as you go."[13] Hence the great commission is more an attitude than a geographical relocation. We are, as we are going, to be looking to make disciples of all nations, baptising them and teaching them to obey. It is this commission to make disciples that summons the church to be an outwardly focused body.

So, the church is *commissioned as a blessed community to be a light to the nations that will attract them to the truth of God as they go about their coming and going.* This is our kingdom work.

The early churches expressed their outward focus through both teaching of the word and by deeds of service. Tertullian in critiquing the philosophers of the second century said, "And yet their words do not find so many disciples as Christians do, who teach not by word, but by deed."[14]

The practice of hospitality[15] was a particularly important expression of the good deeds of the early churches. The New Testament Greek word usually translated hospitality is *philoxenia*. It is composed of two Greek words, *phileo* and *xenos*. *Phileo* is the love or affection for people who are connected by family or faith while *xenos* generally denotes a "stranger." The words for friend and stranger are joined together in hospitality. In Hebrews 13:1-2 *philoxenos* is set alongside "love of brother" (*philadelphia*):

> Let mutual love (*philadelphia*) continue. Do not neglect to show hospitality (*philoxenos*) to strangers.

Therefore, Paul directed his readers to "practice hospitality." (Rom 12:13). Bishops, elders and widows were required to show hospitality (1 Tim 3:2; 5:9-10; Tit 1:8). Disciples received others into their homes (e.g., Acts 2:44-47, 16:15; Rom 16:23; 3 John 5-8). Because new believers came from many backgrounds, the shared meals were useful for building unity and a new identity, for transcending social and ethnic differences, and for making sure that the poor were fed (e.g., Acts 2:46; 1 Cor 11:17-34): hospitality was practically necessary and theologically central.[16]

This concern for theologically grounded mission was taken up by the 12th century Italian nobleman turned monk, Francis of Assisi, who was reported to have urged his followers to "Preach the gospel at all times; when necessary, use words." Although it's unlikely that he actually said this,[17] it does highlight a false dichotomy between "words" and "deeds" when it comes to the gospel. For the first part of the 20th century the Western church was somewhat divided over the methodology of engagement with those outside the church. The liberal, ecumenical, "social gospel" focused on manifesting the kingdom of God on earth by improving human welfare while the Word-focussed gospel emphasised preparing people for the future kingdom by highlighting the need for a personal response to the gospel.[18]

However, in 1974 at the instigation of Billy Graham and John Stott, the Lausanne conference in section 6 on "the Church and Evangelism" sought to address this dichotomy between words and deeds:

> In the Church's mission of sacrificial service, evangelism is primary. World evangelization requires the whole Church to take the whole gospel to the whole world.[19]

The language of the "whole gospel" implies that there is no tension or distinction between words and deeds. As we have seen, Jesus proclaimed, enacted and embodied the gospel of the kingdom as he went about his mission, and the Church is called to do likewise. So, Paul teaches in Colossians 3:17:

> And whatever you do, whether in word or deed, do it all in the name of the Lord Jesus, giving thanks to God the Father through him.

Whatever the local church does, and wherever the members of the church are, they are called to use words and deeds, overflowing from their own sense of blessing and community, to shed the light of Jesus Christ on those around them and invite them to experience the hospitality of the kingdom.

Reflection Questions 3.2
1) What does this survey of theology and church history tell you about outward focus?

2) What does this survey of theology and church history tell you about *your* church's outward focus?

Step 3: Wisdom

Cronshaw et al.[20] researched outwardly focused churches within the Baptist Union of Victoria which had a high proportion of respondents who had a willingness to invite someone to church and a readiness to share their faith with others. Those who were most likely to say they felt at ease talking about their faith, and look for opportunities to do so, also indicated that they were:

- Experiencing personal growth in faith.
- Highly involved in church life.
- Helping people in practical ways.

This would suggest that when a person is helping people in practical ways, they find it easier to share their faith with others because they are experiencing personal growth in their own faith, likely because of their high involvement in church life. In whatever way these factors interact, they produce a positive cycle of personal growth, church involvement and outward focus. Cronshaw's research also identified prayer as a crucial factor in the willingness of believers to share their faith and invite others to church. Gaining God's perspective on people and their circumstances bolsters our concern for them and our conviction that God longs for them to enter his kingdom.

When asked why they would *not* be likely to invite someone to church, the highest ranked response was "those I could invite may not be interested."[21] However, the 2017 research by the McCrindle organisation has identified that more than half of Australians (52%) are "open, to some extent, to changing their religious views given the right circumstances and evidence."[22] Australians identify having conversations and observing people living out a genuine faith as the greatest stimulants to think about spiritual or religious things. For those who know at least one Christian, the top words used to describe Christians were caring, loving and kind. Although

Australian society has changed much in its attitude towards the Church in recent decades, a good number of Australians are still open to investigate Christian spirituality through conversation with a Christian they know.

In light of this reality churches should continue to seek to be "hospitable" and so "invitational." Churches with high levels of newcomers to the Christian faith are more likely to have people who invite non-Christians to participate in church-based activities.[23] Additionally, inviting people to participate in evangelistic courses like *Two Ways to Live*,[24] *Alpha*,[25] and Crossway Baptist church's *Discovery Bible Method*,[26] remains an important part of a church's outward focus. These courses not only provide a way for non-Christians to encounter the gospel, but their promotion in church life prompts the entire congregation to be more outwardly focused.

However, others say that these more traditional modes of outreach are less effective in the post Christian culture. In response to the decline of the church in the Western world and a greater understanding of the missional focus of the Bible, the Missional Church movement has emerged.[27] Two emphases of this movement have been widely accepted by the Western Church. The first is the idea that churches should be incarnational rather than attractional. Jesus was incarnational, entering the world he was seeking to reach. Incarnation includes the notions of presence, proximity, powerlessness, and proclamation.[28] In the same way, believers should seek to live as incarnations of the kingdom in the world and share its gospel in the ordinary rhythms of life, friendship, and community. This is in contrast to the attractional church model which focuses on inviting people to come to church programs as a way to engage them with the gospel.

Missional church advocates also call for a breaking down of the "sacred-secular divide." This is the idea that some things and places, like Sunday worship, are "sacred" and of crucial importance to Christians, while other things, like work, are secular, and less important. The influence of this idea in churches is reflected by the language they use. Pastors and other employed church workers are the only ones who do "ministry" and only those people who preach the gospel in another country are on "mission."

Emerging from the Missional Church focus have been the whole life discipleship and faith-work integration movements. The famous quote by Dorothy L Sayers, though dating from well before the emergence of the Missional Church movement, sums up the underlying philosophy of the whole life discipleship movement well:

> How can any one remain interested in a religion which seems to have no concern with nine-tenths of his life? The Church's approach to an intelligent carpenter is usually confined to exhorting him not to be drunk and disorderly in his leisure hours, and to come to church on Sundays. What the Church should be telling him is this: that the very first demand that his religion makes upon him is that he should make good tables.[29]

One of the symptoms of an inwardly focused church has been an apathy towards the ministry that all Christians perform on their "frontlines"[30] — workplaces, families, social groups, schools etc — beyond the income they produce to give to the church or the specific times when they "share the gospel." Our God creates, grows, builds, heals, teaches, does justice, and serves, and as God's people work with God in their everyday vocations, God's kingdom comes. The idea that God can be as powerfully at work in the workplace as in church on a Sunday morning is a profound awakening for many Christians and a driver of an outward focus. It is so much easier to share the gospel when God's people see themselves already participating in God's kingdom work. For church leaders the main challenge lies in the subtle but important shift in thinking that occurs when new people come to church. Is the first question in the church leader's mind, "How will you best be able to serve the church?" Or is it, "How can the church best serve you in your frontline ministry for the sake of the kingdom?"

Although not all churches will be comfortable with the spectrum of ideas emerging from the Missional or Emerging church movements, some of their ideas have been very helpful in enabling mainstream churches to be more outwardly focused. There is a balance to be found between churches running events which can *attract* non-believers, and mobilising Christians to *incarnate* the gospel of the kingdom in their various frontlines. There is also a balance to be found between ministry performed as individual *scattered* Christians and as *gathered* Christians through corporate church ministries. Yes, evangelism is something we should be doing individually on our frontlines, but we should always feel as though we are part of the larger body of church members doing ministry and mission together.

Reflection Questions 3.3

1) What does this survey of human wisdom tell you about outward focus?

2) What does this survey of human wisdom tell you about *your* church's outward focus?

Step 4: Orthopraxy

The survey of Scripture, tradition and wisdom would suggest that there are at least three things that churches can do to be more outwardly focused.

Missional Hospitality

In light of the biblical imperatives and its wide emphasis during church history, Australian churches should consider the potential of missional hospitality to foster outward focus. Domestic hospitality provides the ideal venue for sharing the gospel of the kingdom in both word and deed. Many churches have a strong culture of sharing meals together, but the challenge is for this hospitality not only to be for Christian friends, but for "strangers" to experience a "taste" of the kingdom. Perhaps churches could commit to encouraging everyone to offer domestic hospitality to non-Christians each month.

Word and Deed

Second, churches need to strike the balance between "word" and "deed" forms of outreach. The faithful proclamation of the whole gospel entails both good deeds and bold proclamation of the gospel message. Proclamation and action are mutually interpretive. Proclamation of the gospel of the kingdom without practical care and concern will sound hollow to a world in need. Yet enacting the kingdom also requires, at the right time and with the right tone, an explanation which enables people to understand the "why" of what we do. And, if our attempts to integrate word and deed are not to ring hollow as just another marketing ploy, they must stem from an authentic concern borne out of the crucible of prayerful intercession and the witness of genuine gospel community.

Gathered and Scattered

There is debate about whether it is better to focus on gathered church-based outreach programs, or on equipping scattered believers for personal evangelism. The answer is — both. A church's ministry programs not only provide the opportunity for some people to be involved in evangelism where they otherwise wouldn't be, but it also promotes the importance of an outward focus across the church and provides impetus for people to be more actively involved in individual evangelism as well.[31]

Both deed and word ministry can be done either at the church or individual level. A Christian can be involved in outreach both through serving at a church soup kitchen or by cooking a meal for their next-door neighbour. They can invite somebody to hear an evangelistic message at their church or they can share the gospel themselves. Churches should seek to strike the balance between corporate word and deed ministry done at the church building and individual word and deed ministry performed by individual Christians on their frontlines.

Reflection Questions 3.4

1) What do you feel is the most important insight on outward focus generated by this chapter?

2) What do you feel is the most important insight on outward focus *for your church* generated by this chapter?

3) What else could your church do to foster a stronger outward focus?

Step 5: Action

Maintaining an outward focus is a particularly difficult challenge for churches in 21st-century Australia. It is an especially complex problem. So it is even more important that we are diligent and intentional in fostering this crucial aspect of church vitality.

Here is a process which you might like to use or adapt to develop some action steps to foster outward focus in your church:

1) Gather together as a leadership and pray for the discernment of God's wisdom for your church with respect to its outward focus, or lack thereof.

2) Share together your answers to Reflection Questions 3.4.

3) Individually, write down your answer to the following question: What should our church *do* to foster outward focus? You might come up with up to five suggestions. Try to make your suggestions as specific as possible. For example, rather than just saying "Foster a sense of outward focus in the church," you could suggest something like "Hold four 'Hospitality Sundays' during the year," or "Run an Alpha course."

4) Go around the group and have each member suggest one action the church could take to foster a stronger outward focus. Write the suggestion on a whiteboard or similar media. If your suggestion has already been made put a tick next to it on the whiteboard and then share your next suggestion.

5) When everyone has shared all of their suggestions, each member in the group is allocated three votes. (You might like to allocate each member three self-adhesive dots for this activity.) Each member can then use their votes. They can allocate all three votes to the same suggestion or utilise them across a number of suggestions.

6) Tally up the dots and you will have an indication of what, as a leadership team, might be a good action step to take to develop a stronger outward focus in your church. Pray again and then decide which action steps you wish to take. Two or three is probably all that you can attempt at one time. Keep a record of your suggestions because you may be able to come back to them next year.

Conclusion

In one of the most important of Jesus' kingdom parables he tells the story of a sower casting seed onto different types of soil. The seed is the gospel of the kingdom, and the soil is the heart of those who are exposed to it. Some are hardhearted, some are shallow, some are choked by the Deceiver and the concerns of this world – and you might well think it's a pretty discouraging parable up to this point! However, Jesus' emphasis is that some of the seed lands in fertile soil and bears kingdom fruit thirty-fold, sixty-fold and a hundred-fold. It only takes one seed to bear fruit to make it all worthwhile. Evangelism in Australia is tough work at the moment but, in God's faithfulness, the promise of the fruitfulness of the gospel will endure as our churches intentionally and diligently maintain their outward focus.

Chapter Endnotes

1. Quoted in W. Vaus and D. Gresham, *Mere Theology: A Guide to the Thought of C. S. Lewis* (Downers Grove; Leicester: InterVarsity Press, 2004), 167.

2. Scott B. McKee, "The Relationship between Church Health and Church Growth in the Evangelical Presbyterian Church" (Doctor of Ministry Dissertation. Asbury Theological Seminary, 2003).

3. Ed Stetzer and Thom S. Rainer, *Transformational Church: Creating a New Scorecard for Congregations* (Nashville: B&H Publishing Group, 2010).

4. Christian A. Schwarz, *Natural Church Development: A Guide to Eight Essential Qualities of Healthy Churches (7th Updated and Revised Edition)* (St. Charles: Churchsmart Resources, 2006).

5. Diana Butler Bass, *Christianity for the Rest of Us: How the Neighborhood Church Is Transforming the Faith* (New York: HarperOne, 2009).

6. Linda Bobbitt, "Measuring Congregational Vitality: Phase 2 Development of an Outcome Measurement Tool," *Review of Religious Research* 56, no. 3 (2014).

7. Ruth Powell et al., *Enriching Church Life*, 2nd ed. (St Mary's: Mirrabooka Press & NCLS Research, 2012).

8. Cynthia Woolever and Deborah Bruce, *Beyond the Ordinary: Ten Strengths of Us Congregations* (Louisville: Westminster John Knox Press, 2004).

9. See, for example, Anne Klose, *Covenantal Priesthood: A Narrative of Community for Baptist Churches* (Carlisle: Paternoster, 2018), 173-79.

10 Christopher J.H. Wright, *The Mission of God's People: A Biblical Theology of the Church's Mission* (Grand Rapids: Zondervan, 2010), 68.

11 Eddie Gibbs and Ryan Bolger, *Emerging Churches: Creating Christian Community in Postmodern Culture* (London: SPCK, 2006), 125.

12 C. René Padilla, "The Mission of the Church in Light of the Kingdom of God," *Transformation* 1, no. 2 (1984): 18.

13 Robert D. Culver, "What Is the Church's Commission? Some Exegetical Issues in Matthew 28: 16-20," *Bibliotheca Sacra* 125, no. 499 (1968).

14 Tertullian *Defense* Trans. Rev. S. Thelwall. 50.14

15 Hospitality should be thought of as the act of being friendly and welcoming to guests rather than just sharing meals together, although eating together is a powerful expression of hospitality.

16 Christine D. Pohl, "Building a Place for Hospitality," in *Hospitality*, ed. Robert B. Kruschwitz (Waco: The Center for Christian Ethics Baylor University, 2007), 29.

17 Mark Galli, "Speak the Gospel," *Christianity Today* May 21, 2009 (2009).

18 Wilbert R. Shenk, "The Whole Is Greater Than the Sum of the Parts: Moving Beyond Word and Deed," *Missiology* 21, no. 1 (1993).

19 https://www.lausanne.org/content/covenant/lausanne-covenant#cov

20 Darren Cronshaw et al., "Churches Who Share Their Faith: A Case Study Survey of the Baptist Union of Victoria," *Australian e-journal of Theology* 22, no. 2 (2015).

21 Ibid., 104.

22 Mark McCrindle, *Faith and Belief in Australia* (Sydney: McCrindle Research Pty Ltd, 2017), 9.

23 Powell et al., 56.

24 https://www.twowaystolive.com/2wtl/whowillbeking/

25 https://www.alpha.org.au/

26 https://www.crossway.org.au/dbm/

27 See Michael Frost and Alan Hirsch, *The Shaping of Things to Come* (Peabody: Hendrickson, 2003); Darrell L Guder and Lois Barrett, *Missional Church: A Vision for the Sending of the Church in North America* (Grand Rapids: Wm. B. Eerdmans Publishing, 1998); Lesslie Newbigin, *Foolishness to the Greeks: The Gospel and Western Culture* (Grand Rapids: Wm. B. Eerdmans Publishing, 1986).

28 Kim Hammond and Darren Cronshaw, *Sentness: Six Postures of Missional Christians* (Downers Grove: InterVarsity Press, 2014).

29 Dorothy L. Sayers, "Why Work?," in *Creed or Chaos* (New York: Harcourt Brace, 1949), 7.

30 Mark Greene, *Fruitfulness on the Frontline: Making a Difference Where You Are* (Nottingham: IVP, 2014).

31 Peter Kaldor, John Bellamy, and Sandra Moore, *Mission under the Microscope: Keys to Effective and Sustainable Mission* (Adelaide: Openbook, 1995), 48.

Chapter 4
Empowering Leadership

Introduction

Leadership is undoubtedly one of the most exhaustively (and exhaustingly!) explored topics in the Western world in the 21st century. Google the term and you will find a bewildering number of books, articles, blogs, videos and podcasts about leadership. Why? People recognise that leadership is crucial to the flourishing of every aspect of our societies, from families to organisations and nations.

We begin here by affirming that godly forms of leadership are also vital for every church as they pursue their kingdom aligned vision. As we pointed out in our chapter on developing such vision, kingdom aligned ends can only be served by kingdom shaped means and this is nowhere truer than in relation to leadership. As we'll see, Jesus provides the perfect model of such kingdom aligned leadership but, encouragingly, this kingdom congruence is also borne out in the research into vitality-engendering forms of church leadership. Descriptors of such church leadership include "visionary," "caring," "inspirational," and even "courageous," but the term most used by researchers to describe leadership in vital and healthy churches is "empowering."[1]

Given this finding, and our kingdom focus, we need to unpack some all-too familiar terms in some not-so-familiar ways. Starting to grasp how we use these terms as they relate to the local church context will help you navigate your way through this chapter:

- Power: the capacity to achieve kingdom aligned ends by kingdom shaped means

- Authority: the God-given and church-endorsed[2] warrant and responsibility to exercise such power
- Relational power: the capacity to achieve kingdom aligned ends through influencing others
- Leaders are those:
  - with a firm grasp on their church's kingdom aligned vision and a commitment to the kingdom shaped means by which it is seeks to achieve this vision
  - who, according to their own gifting, calling and the needs of the church, exercise their own power
  - with authority
  - and enable and equip others to exercise their power.

Hopefully, it is clear from these definitions that *servant* leadership of the kind modelled by Jesus is not one option among many. In Christian terms, servant leadership is the only form on offer because leadership exists only to *serve* God and one another as we fulfill God's kingdom purposes. This is not to deny the complexities and pitfalls of empowering leadership which we'll be exploring below. But it does give us hope that we begin with a clear kingdom focus which will keep on us track.

Step 1: Context

Firstly, we need to recognise that the exercise of leadership in your church will depend considerably on the church tradition to which you belong. Some churches, such as those of the Anglican Communion, can be described as "hierarchical." You have a well-defined leadership structure which determines how power and authority are distributed and used. There may be more power vested in the denominational hierarchy than in the local church. At the other end of the spectrum, some churches are autonomous with congregational forms of government. These churches locate the centre of authority in the church membership. In other churches power is focused in a small group of leaders. This is often called a "presbyterian" church structure even though you may not be Presbyterian! It is worthwhile reflecting on the leadership structure of your church and what this means in terms of navigating your way through the various issues and questions we raise.

Next, one of the core qualities of the National Church Life Survey is "Inspiring and Empowering Leadership." If you have recently completed the NCLS this will be a great place for you to start as you explore your own particular context.

And finally, in their widely recognised research into empowering leadership behaviours, Josh Arnold and his colleagues highlighted eight leadership behaviours which team members identified as being empowering.[3] These behaviours serve as a useful tool for reflection. In light of these findings, you might like to fill in the following table which suggests some empowering behaviours that you, as a leadership team, may have exercised in your church in the last 12 months.

Empowering Behaviour	Where our leadership team have done this in the last 12 months
1) The church has seen us leading by example	
2) We are coaching groups or individuals in the church	
3) We are encouraging groups or individuals in the church	
4) We exercise participative decision-making	
5) We inform groups or individuals in the church about decisions or policy changes	
6) We show concern for groups or individuals in the church	
7) We interact with groups or individuals within the church as a leadership	

8) We help develop relationships in groups within the church as a leadership	

Reflection questions 4.1
1) What do the NCLS results tell you about the level of empowering leadership in your church?

2) What are your reflections on completing the empowering behaviour chart above?

3) What other evidence do you have that you are an empowering leadership team?

Step 2: Scripture and Tradition

The kingdom, as we have already explored, is God's from beginning to end and his capacity to achieve all that it entails is perfect and complete. He is all-powerful. At every turn in human history — in creation, through Israel, quintessentially in the life, death and resurrection of his Son, through the Church and in the yet to come fulfilment of the kingdom — God has and is continuing to powerfully work out his kingdom purposes. The completion of this work is absolutely assured.

In the Old Testament we learn that the world is created and sustained by this power (Ps 148:4; 65:5-8), and that same power is demonstrated by deeds of deliverance performed by God's mighty hand and outstretched arm (Exod 15:6; Deut 5:15; Ps 111:6). In this context, God empowers humanity and delegates his authority to them in creation:

> [26] Then God said, "Let us make mankind in our image, in our likeness, so that they may rule over the fish in the sea and the birds in the sky, over the livestock and all the wild animals, and over all the creatures that move along the ground." (Gen 1:26)

And this pattern continues through his appointment and empowering of leaders like Moses, Deborah, David and Nehemiah (Exod 4:10-12; Judg 4:4-10; 1 Sam 16:1-13; Neh 1-2).

In the New Testament, as we have already seen, Jesus comes proclaiming, enacting and embodying the gospel of the kingdom of God. He has received his Father's complete warrant and responsibility to exercise all the power of the kingdom for kingdom purposes (Matt 28:18; Eph 1:20-23). The gospel of who he is and what he achieves "is the power of God for salvation for everyone who has faith" (Rom 1:16). Mark clearly demonstrates that Jesus has God's authority in the early part of his gospel. In rapid succession Jesus is recognised as teaching with astounding authority (1:22); he demonstrates power over evil spirits (1:21-28), sickness (1:29-34), leprosy (uncleanness) (1:40-42) and sin and its consequences (2:1-12). He goes on to demonstrate authority over the Sabbath (2:23-28) and nature itself (4:31-41). In all this, Jesus entirely rejects any means of exercising his power which is not aligned with the nature of the kingdom: in his rejection of Satan's temptations (Luke 4:1-12); through his teaching of his disciples (Matt 18:1-5; 20:20-28); in his demonstration of humble service (John 13:3-20); and culminating in his most powerful moment-achieving kingdom ends by kingdom means – on the cross (Mark 10:45; Phil 2:1-11).

From the outset of his ministry, Jesus is also intent on empowering his disciples. He grants them "power and authority over all the demons and to heal diseases" and commissions them "to proclaim the kingdom of God" (Luke 9:1-2). In the context of discernment within the church, he assures them of his authoritative presence and heaven's backing (Matt 18:17-20), and he empowers them despite their sin and frailty (John 21:15-17). He also empowers the weakest and most marginalised in Jewish society. Women are empowered to learn and bear witness (John 4:28-30; Matt 28:7); those who are healed or delivered are enabled for productive work and their place in community; and children are blessed and dignified as examples of kingdom life.

Then, at the end of Jesus' earthly ministry, he ushers in a radical form of empowerment in the person of the Holy Spirit:

> [8] But you will receive power when the Holy Spirit comes on you; and you will be my witnesses in Jerusalem, and in all Judea and Samaria, and to the ends of the earth. (Acts 1:8)

This Spirit would empower his disciples to share the gospel of the kingdom (Acts 2:1-42); to live transformed lives (Rom 15:13; Gal 5:16-26); to exercise the gifts of the Spirit (1 Cor 12:1-11); to live in the unity of Christ's body (1 Cor 12: 12-13); and to finally receive the fullness of kingdom life at the resurrection (Rom 8:11).

In this context, Paul prays that the church will come to understand and appreciate the immense power it possesses:

> [18] I pray that the eyes of your heart may be enlightened in order that you may know the hope to which he has called you, the riches of his glorious inheritance in his holy people, [19] and his incomparably great power for us who believe. That power is the same as the mighty strength [20] he exerted when he raised Christ from the dead and seated him at his right hand in the heavenly realms... (Eph 1:18-22)

The way in which this power is to be exercised, especially by leaders, is reflected by Paul's correspondence with Timothy in his leadership role in the church at Ephesus:

> For God has not given us a spirit of timidity, but of power and love and discipline. (2 Tim 1:7)

Timothy is not to abandon his power but to use it with love for the good of those he leads – achieving kingdom ends by kingdom means. Peter also encourages his fellow leaders to exercise oversight of their flocks with kingdom motives:

> Therefore, I exhort the elders among you, as your fellow elder and witness of the sufferings of Christ, and a partaker also of the glory that is to be revealed, [2]shepherd the flock of God among you, exercising oversight not under compulsion, but voluntarily, according to the will of God; and not for sordid gain, but with eagerness; [3]nor yet as lording it over those allotted to your charge, but proving to be examples to the flock. (1 Pet 5:1-3 (NASB))

In particular, church leaders should use the gifts with which God has empowered them to equip and empower other members of the church:

> [11] So Christ himself gave the apostles, the prophets, the evangelists, the pastors and teachers, [12] to equip his people for works of service, so that the body of Christ may be built up. (Eph 4:11-12)

God's whole enterprise of entrusting power and authority to ordinary women and men, albeit those who are redeemed and empowered by the Spirit, appears unconscionably risky. If we were God, we probably wouldn't go about something as important as the kingdom in this way! But God does — and calls us, with due care, to do likewise as we empower others. This insight means that we must be able to accept and even expect failure — our own and other's — just as God does.

And finally, while there are certainly times of great joy in exercising Christian leadership, we provide a health warning because leadership like that of Christ inevitably entails joining in his suffering. This happens, not because God's kingdom power has somehow failed us, but for his glory as, in our suffering, we continue to proclaim, enact and embody the gospel of the sure and coming kingdom (Col 1:24). According to Jesus himself, the shepherd "lays down his life for the sheep" (John 10:11) and Paul, following in Jesus' footsteps declares:

> [10] I want to know Christ—yes, to know the power of his resurrection and participation in his sufferings, becoming like him in his death, [11] and so, somehow, attaining to the resurrection from the dead. (Phil 3:10-11; see also Col 1: 11-14)

This challenging association of leadership, power and suffering may explain but can by no means excuse the awful failings of leadership which are strewn across the pages of church history. Every exercise of power by God's people for other than kingdom ends, or by other than kingdom means, is a betrayal of that kingdom, its gospel and the one who died for us.

From the time when Constantine painted the cross on the shields of his soldiers as they went into battle, the Church has often lapsed into the use of coercion, even violence, to further its alleged cause.[4] Catholics burnt Protestants, Protestants burnt Catholics, and church authorities of both persuasions drowned Anabaptists! Church leaders aligned themselves with systems of secular and political power, interposed themselves between God and his people, and prohibited them from reading God's word. More recently we have seen the abuse of power sink to the depths of sexual predation and donning the garb of Bible-toting righteousness to exert tyrannical control over "the flock." But there is hope.

In every generation God *has* faithfully raised up leaders who are firmly committed to the exercise of their power for kingdom ends by kingdom means — and many have suffered for it. None of them were perfect but this fact is perhaps an encouragement to us in our own attempts to lead well. Dietrich Bonhoeffer (1906-1945) was just such a leader. Destined for a stellar academic career, he chose to take a stand against the idolatrous leadership offered to the German people by Adolf Hitler,[5] and, despite several opportunities to escape Germany, chose to remain as a servant leader to his fellow Christians. In particular, he lived and taught in Christian community at a clandestine seminary in Finkenwalde (1935-1937), where he shunned the temptation of becoming sole leader, rather setting down rhythms of life and spiritual practices which emphasised mutuality and empowerment, and placed a constant focus on Christ alone as their Lord and Saviour.[6] Bonhoeffer had remained committed to pacifist forms of resistance but, as the war dragged on and the Holocaust gained momentum, concluded that he could not ethically resile from more direct forms of action which culminated in an unsuccessful plot to assassinate Hitler.[7] There was no doubt that Bonhoeffer was committed to kingdom purposes, but were these kingdom means? Those of us who have not faced such awful dilemmas are ill-qualified to judge, but we can most certainly learn from his careful wrestling with his responsibilities to God and those he led. Bonhoeffer was hanged in Flossenberg concentration camp in April 1945 and is remembered as a Christian martyr.

Reflection Questions 4.2
1) What does this survey of theology and church history tell you about empowering leadership?

2) What does this survey of theology and church history tell you about *your* church's leadership style?

Step 3 Wisdom

On the basis of what we've learnt so far, we need two major forms of resourcing as we explore what wisdom has to say about leadership. We need our leadership to be powerful — in the sense of being effective for kingdom purposes — and servant-shaped. Long term ineffectiveness will sap any congregation's motivation to press on in their kingdom purposes. Failure to love and serve as we lead will sabotage our work and, even worse, discourage people in their faith. Both issues demand our attention.

The need for this balance is repeatedly acknowledged in the research literature (both church and secular) on leadership.

Christian Schwartz, for example, identifies that although goal orientation is a significant leadership trait for church health, a "people orientation" is equally or more important.[8] His Natural Church Development (NCD) research suggests that the crucial focus of local church leadership should be the development of people. Running programs and ensuring compliance with government and denominational regulations is important, but the essential work of church leadership is discipleship — empowering others to live kingdom lives shaped lives in kingdom shaped churches.

Similarly, in discussing their core quality of Empowering Leadership, the National Church Life Survey team highlight the importance of leaders developing the gifts and skills of congregational members. Leadership which focuses on helping church members to identify their gifts and skills is strongly correlated with church growth and the percentage of newcomers who come and remain. This intriguing connection points to the vital place of empowering leadership in church life.[9]

The management literature identifies two dimensions of empowering leadership. Power is shared through the organisation, first through formal organisational practices, and second, through techniques to enhance personal efficacy, motivation or commitment.[10] In other words, empowerment involves both a structure that shares authority and the personal encouragement of organisation members to have the confidence to use that authority. Empowering leadership has both policy and relational dimensions. Both must be in place for people to be properly empowered.

With a focus on relational practices, Arnold et al. (as mentioned in Section 1) have developed a model of empowering leadership based on their research into leadership behaviours within high performing teams. Such behaviours include:[11]

1) **Leading by example:** showing the leader's commitment to their own work as well as the work of others.

2) **Coaching:** educating team members and helping them become self-reliant. This includes making suggestions about performance improvements, helping the team to be self-reliant and helping others see areas where they need more training.
3) **Encouraging:** acknowledging team efforts and encouraging team members to solve problems together.
4) **Participative decision making:** leader's engaging with team members' input in making decisions.
5) **Informing:** explaining decisions to the team and informing them about new developments in organizational policy.
6) **Showing concern:** showing regard for team members' well-being, taking time to discuss concerns, and treating group members with respect.
7) **Interacting with the team:** keeping track of what is going on in the team.
8) **Group management:** helping to develop good relations among work group members and suggesting that team members evaluate their own work.

This model is based on work teams in business contexts but, we would suggest, provides useful ideas for *how* to be loving and empowering leaders.

Finally, a word about accountability in leadership. As we have already flagged, the exercise of power associated with leadership is a risky business and we need to be well informed and resourced in mitigating such risks. Richard Gula, for example, has provided a thorough examination of what it means to undertake *Just Ministry*,[12] while Peter Scazzero provides a more personal approach to such issues in *The Emotionally Healthy Leader*, particularly alerting us to the many forms of interpersonal power, some of which we may not even be aware we possess.[13] Accountability is vital to enable us to identify those areas in which we need to continue to grow in effectiveness, become aware of our blind spots and be alert to our vulnerabilities. Various professions have taken up this challenge to encourage growth in effectiveness, self-awareness in practice and adherence to ethical (and we would add kingdom) methods, through supervisory and other supportive processes.[14]

Reflection Questions 4.3

1) What does this survey of human wisdom tell you about empowering leadership?

2) What does this survey of human wisdom tell you about *your* church's leadership style?

Step 4 Orthopraxy

As always, our task in this section is to bring together the findings of this chapter so far in a set of practical principles for *right practice* with respect to leadership.

Servant Leadership

First, we must recognise that leadership and power belong, in an ultimate sense, to God alone. He has fulfilled, he is fulfilling, and he will fulfill his kingdom purposes. All our endeavours rest on this complete assurance, so that while we should work hard to play our part in such purposes, we can do so with a calm confidence that God's got this! We should be prayerfully expectant that his power will be at work in our churches.

But, we have also seen that kingdom power (for kingdom aligned purposes by kingdom shaped means) is only ours as God delegates it to us. It is neither a right nor something of our own, but a responsibility which he authorises us to exercise. Our churches have a role to play in attentively recognising and endorsing such authority, though how this occurs will depend on our leadership structures.

As Jesus modelled for us, such leadership will always be servant hearted. In kingdom terms, there are no alternative forms of leadership. Leadership exists only to serve God and others. In these terms, power is a good gift from God, and we should seek to increase its right practice in ourselves, and others.

Given the intoxicating nature of power, and the well documented cases where church leaderships have failed to use power as servants, we all need to be alert to its dangers. Sometimes we pursue kingdom ends but not utilising kingdom means. Church leaderships should be constantly checking that they are using their delegated power as servants, not as "lords" (Matt 20:25). Such power check-ups should involve both rigourous self-scrutiny and input from those outside the leadership. Normally, nobody will force you to do this. For leaderships to allow their use of power to be scrutinised is purely an exercise in humility and obedience. But we pray this is a servant leadership posture that you are willing to adopt.

Empowering Leadership

Our own power (or rather God's power in us) is not diminished when we share it with others, but rather expands for God's glory. Such empowering leadership is risky and may lead to missteps, but God is with us through it all. Our organisational structures and processes should empower everyone within our church communities to exercise their capacity to fulfill kingdom purposes by kingdom means. Within our more formal layers of leadership, such empowerment means the decentralisation of decision making and sharing the authority and resources (financial, material, personnel) necessary to enact such decisions. The confidence to do this rests in God's faithfulness and the knowledge that your church's kingdom vision has been shared with and is supported by your congregational leaders (see Chapter 1). Even if they do things in very different ways from yours, you will be on the same kingdom page and can continue to work out your differences on this basis. There should also be a strong emphasis on helping people identify their gifts and skills, and developing opportunities to use these for the kingdom.

But no matter how well our organisational structures and processes are working, we will come unstuck if the interpersonal means by which we seek to carry them out fail to enact the characteristics of kingdom community. Again, there may be ideas and skills to learn and adapt from secular research and experience, but this is the bread and butter of being church. Empowering leadership is fundamentally an interpersonal activity providing church members with the confidence to utilise the empowering structures that the church leadership have put in place to grow in their capacity to achieve kingdom ends by kingdom means.

This last point is beautifully illustrated by an example from another culture. Apparently, in Sudanese communities, on the first day when a visitor arrives they are given a meal and a bed, on the second day this is repeated, but on the third day they are given a hoe![15] Following this principle, churches should be looking to involve new people in ministry as quickly as possible.[16] Not only does this mean they begin using their skills and gifts in the service of God and his church, but they quickly develop a strong sense of belonging and ownership. Further, their rapid involvement in ministry becomes their expectation of the norm. Church life does not mean just consuming but is always a life of service. Clearly new people to church will not be preaching or leading worship, but churches need to work hard to identify and develop simple ministry activities that anybody can perform. There need to be clear pathways whereby everyone in the church community can identify and develop their spiritual gifts, skills and resources and be empowered to play their part for God's kingdom.

Finally, all this must be safe guarded by accountability in our leadership and the exercise of its associated forms of power. This may range from formal processes such as vigorous pastoral supervision, whether by elderships or professional supervisors, to mentoring, coaching and discipleship at various levels of intensity. Robust relationships which are both warmly relational and yet willing to address areas in need of growth, blind spots and vulnerabilities will keep us all on track.

Reflection Questions 4.4
1) How are servant leadership and empowering leadership already at work in your church?

2) Which of the principles of orthopraxis discussed above are most in need of your attention as a leadership?

Step 5: Action

Developing action steps related to empowering leadership is probably the most challenging exercise you undertake as part of your Practical Theology because it focuses largely on yourselves as a leadership. This dynamic means that you may need the assistance of an external consultant to help you gain a clear view of how leadership is functioning in your church, both its strengths and challenges. At the very least, you will need to provide safe and encouraging processes to receive feedback from the people you lead about whether and how your leadership empowers them.

Here is a process which you might like to use or adapt to develop some action steps towards empowering leadership in your church:

1) Gather together as a leadership and pray for the discernment of God's wisdom for your church with respect to your leadership.

2) Share together your answers to Reflection Question 4.

3) Individually, write down your answer to the following question: What should we do, as leadership, to be more servant hearted and empowering of the people we have been entrusted to lead? You might come up with up to five suggestions. Try to make your suggestions as specific as possible. For example, rather than just saying "Be more empowering," you could suggest something like "Invite a different ministry team to our leaders meeting each month to hear what they are doing and to encourage and pray for them" or "Run a course on spiritual gifts each year."

4) Go around the group and have each member suggest one action the church could take to be a more servant hearted and empowering leadership. Write the suggestion on a whiteboard or similar media. If your suggestion has already been made put a tick next to it on the whiteboard and then share your next suggestion.

5) When everyone has shared all of their suggestions, each member in the group is allocated three votes. (You might like to allocate each member three self-adhesive dots for this activity.) Each member can then use their votes. They can allocate all three votes to the same suggestion or utilise them across a number of suggestions.

6) Tally up the dots and you will have an indication of what, as a leadership team, might be a good action step to take to be more servant hearted and empowering. Pray again and then decide which action steps you wish to take. Two or three is probably all that you can attempt at one time. Keep a record of your suggestions because you may be able to come back to them next year.

Conclusion

Leadership can be daunting and demanding. We take our confidence from God's perfect capacity to achieve his kingdom aligned purposes by his kingdom shaped means — and if we are ever in doubt as to what this looks like, we have the perfect example of Jesus Christ. Meditating on him – his life, his ministry, his death and resurrection, his presence with us by his Spirit, and his impending return in glory – will transform everything about us, especially our leadership. Jesus delegates his power and authority to us, his people, as together we live kingdom shapes lives in kingdom shaped churches. And we are most powerful when we empower others.

Chapter Endnotes

1. Christian Schwarz, *Natural Church Development* (Emmelsbull: C. and P. Publishing, 1996), 22; Cynthia Woolever and Deborah Bruce, *Beyond the Ordinary: Ten Strengths of Us Congregations* (Louisville: Westminster John Knox Press, 2004); Scott B McKee, "The Relationship between Church Health and Church Growth in the Evangelical Presbyterian Church" (Doctor of Ministry Dissertation. Asbury Theological Seminary, 2003); Ruth Powell et al., *Enriching Church Life*, 2nd ed. (Saint Mary's: Mirrabooka Press & NCLS Research, 2012).

2. Such endorsement may be formal (requiring appointment through due process) or informal (recognition in some way within the congregation of this person's capacity and calling).

3. Josh A. Arnold, Sharon Arad, Jonathan A. Rhoades, and Fritz Drasgow, "The Empowering Leadership Questionnaire: The Construction and Validation of a New Scale for Measuring Leader Behaviors," *Journal of Organizational Behavior* 21 (2000).

4. John P. Dickson, *Bullies and Saints : An Honest Look at the Good and Evil of Christian History* (London: Zondervan, 2021).

5. John D. Godsey, *The Theology of Dietrich Bonhoeffer*, Preacher's Library (London: SCM Press, 1960), 84.

6. See Dietrich Bonhoeffer, *Life Together* (New York: Harper & Row, 1954).

7. Geffrey B. Kelly and Burton Nelson, *The Cost of Moral Leadership: The Spirituality of Dietrich Bonhoeffer* (Grand Rapids: Eerdmans, 2003), 180.

8. Schwarz, 22.

9   Powell et al., 41.

10 Jay A. Conger and Rabindra N. Kanungo, "The Empowerment Process: Integrating Theory and Practice," *Academy of Management Review* 13, no. 3 (1988): 474.

11 Arnold et al., 255.

12 Richard M. Gula, *Just Ministry: Professional Ethics for Pastoral Ministers* (Mahwah: Paulist Press, 2013).

13 Peter Scazzero, *The Emotionally Healthy Leader: How Transforming Your Inner Life Will Deeply Transform Your Church, Team, and the World* (Grand Rapids: Zondervan, 2015), see especially chapter 8.

14 Early work in this area was especially focused on other forms of the caring professions such as counselling and social work. See, for example, Peter Hawkins and Aisling McMahon, *Supervision in the Helping Professions*, 5th edition (London: Open University Press, 2020). But this work has now been thoroughly adapted to pastoral leadership. See, for example, Jane Leach and Michael Paterson, *Pastoral Supervision: A Handbook New Edition*, 2nd ed. (London: SCM Press, 2015).

15 Rosemary Dewerse, *Breaking Calabashes: Becoming an Intercultural Community* (Unley: Mediacom, 2013) quoted in Cronshaw et al, 224.

16 Empowerment must also apply to the ways in which members of our congregation exercise their kingdom power beyond the church. See for example the importance of whole life discipleship and faith-work integration in Chapter 3.

Chapter 5
Vibrant Faith

Introduction

We do hope that by now the vision of God's kingdom is starting to get a firm grip on you - for yourselves and your church. God *is* king, and his kingdom is a realm of unfolding blessing for his people and his world. As Christ came, proclaiming, enacting and embodying the gospel, he *has* inaugurated the kingdom: his kingdom work is not half done, it is finished, and he *does* reign. Therefore, as his Church and his body, though we occupy the "now and not yet" time between Christ's ascension and return, we live and labour under the authority, the protection, the provision and the empowerment of this reign by the power of the Holy Spirit. By living kingdom shaped lives in kingdom shaped churches, we come to act as embassies, or outstations, of the kingdom, and our loving communities communicate the gospel in word and deed to God's world. In doing so, we seek to share the great kingdom blessings with which we have been blessed. And finally, Christ *will* come again in glory as judge and redeemer to perfect and consummate his kingdom. In Christ, we will be God's people and he will be our God, ruling forever in the new heaven and the new earth. This is our certain hope.

The vibrant faith on which we focus in this chapter is nurtured and sustained by this vision, encountered as a living dynamic in our lives. At every level — personal and communal, inward and outward — there is a sense of vibrant growth in living kingdom shaped lives in kingdom shaped churches for God's glory and the sake of his world. Nourished by our devotion to God in Bible reading and prayer, such faith comes alive to God's presence and priority in all we do. This overflows into our participation in God's kingdom shaped community and mission, putting our faith into action. Sharing the stories of the joys and challenges of this in the community of faith, in turn, fuels our devotion to God, renewing us in our kingdom vision. And so on.

This positive cycle is borne out by the research into church vitality which highlights the importance of spirituality, prayer and growing faith. According to the Natural Church Development (NCD) research, the kind of "passionate spirituality" which is related to church vitality depends on "the degree to which faith is actually lived out with commitment, passion and enthusiasm."[1] It is a spirituality experienced, shared and acted upon. Personal practices of prayer and Bible reading are key contributors to its vigour, and these impact and transform every aspect of life, resulting in what the NCLS research terms "Alive and Growing Faith."[2] We think the term "Vibrant Faith" is a good umbrella term for these features of church vitality.[3]

Our aim in this chapter is to enable you to find ways to foster this vibrant faith which work for your church, in your context.

Step One: Context

As with several of our other dimensions, you may need to be aware of the differences between your own reflections on vibrant faith (as those who are strongly committed to God and your church) and those of your wider congregation. Take some time to consider your own responses to the NCD statements listed below – and then think through how other members of your church community might respond to them. Your latest NCLS results regarding "Alive and Growing Faith" will provide a good check on the accuracy of your sense of where your church stands on this.

Reflection questions 5.1

1) Read through the Natural Church Development statements related to passionate spirituality. On a scale of 1 (not very true) to 5 (very true) how true are the statements for you and for your church?

a) I experience God's work in my life

b) I experience the transforming influences faith has in the different areas of my life (profession, family, spare time, etc)

c) I often tell other Christians when I have experienced something from God

d) Times of prayer are an inspiring experience for me

e) I know that other church members pray for me regularly

f) I enjoy reading the Bible on my own

g) The Bible is a powerful guide for me in the decisions of everyday life

h) I am enthusiastic about our church

i) I firmly believe that God will act even more powerfully in our church in coming years

j) Our leaders are spiritual examples to me.

2) The NCLS research measures a core quality called "Alive and Growing Faith." How did your church score in your most recent NCLS survey?

3) How does your church go about developing vibrant faith amongst your congregants?

Step Two: Scripture and Tradition

As always, we want to anchor our exploration of this dimension of church vitality in Scripture. In what terms does the Bible address vibrant faith and what does it teach about how we can best foster it in our churches in service of our kingdom aligned vision?

The Nature of Vibrant Faith

The language of "faith" in the Old Testament is usually associated with the covenant between God and his people.[4] Faith has less to do with a set of ideas or beliefs than it does to being attentive to relationship with God. Only rarely does the Old Testament speak of "faith" as a body of teaching that Israel is to believe. Faith is to "trust in" *someone*, as opposed to *something* to "assent to." Certainly, it involves obedience to Torah (the law) but such obedience stems from a fidelity to relationship with Yahweh. Similarly, faith in the New Testament is about living life in relationship with Christ and in light of that relationship, holding on to the promises of God in Christ for both salvation and for one's day-to-day life.[5] The interplay between a deeply personal trust and fidelity to the truth about God comes alive in Paul's personal testimony to Timothy (2 Tim 1:11-14, emphasis added):

> [11] And of this gospel I was appointed a herald and an apostle and a teacher. [12] That is why I am suffering as I am. Yet this is no cause for shame, because *I know whom I have believed, and am convinced that he is able to guard what I have entrusted to him until that day.* [13] What you heard from me, keep as the pattern of sound teaching, with faith and love in Christ Jesus. [14] Guard the good deposit that was entrusted to you—guard it with the help of the Holy Spirit who lives in us.

In the verses just before these Paul cannot help but restate the wonderful news of the gospel: it is his whole life and calling. But his faith boils down, not to a "what" but a "whom." He has totally entrusted himself to the person of Jesus Christ. Such trust is certainly borne along by "the standard of sound teaching" but, yet again, it centres on "the faith and love that are *in Christ Jesus*."

In scriptural terms, this vibrant faith is undeniably "enthusiastic." This word comes from two Greek words, "*en*," meaning "in," and "*theos*" meaning God. To be en-thusiastic is to be "in God." It is perhaps the type of spirituality that Paul encourages the Romans to have:

> Never be lacking in zeal, but keep your spiritual fervour, serving the Lord (Rom 12:11)

The word translated "fervour" (*zestos*) is literally "boil" or "seethe" and means to be stirred up emotionally, and to be enthusiastic, excited or "on fire."[6] The adjectival form of the same word appears in Revelation 3 where Jesus speaks to the church in Laodicea:

> ¹⁵ I know your deeds, that you are neither cold nor hot (*zeontes*). I wish you were either one or the other! ¹⁶ So, because you are lukewarm—neither hot nor cold—I am about to spit you out of my mouth (Rev 3:15-16).

Enthusiasm or fervour stems from a life empowered by the Holy Spirit and is central to our whole being and purpose as citizens of God's kingdom. The adjective *pneumatikos* (spiritual) refers to qualities produced in persons empowered by God's Spirit:[7]

> ¹² What we have received is not the spirit of the world, but the Spirit who is from God, so that we may understand what God has freely given us. ¹³ This is what we speak, not in words taught us by human wisdom but in words taught by the Spirit, explaining spiritual realities with Spirit-taught words. (1 Cor 2:12-13)

A spiritual life is one which manifests the fruit of the Holy Spirit: "love, joy, peace, patience, kindness, generosity, faithfulness, ²³ gentleness, and self-control" (Gal 5 :22-23). Such a life is also Spirit-gifted and empowered to fulfil God's kingdom purposes by his kingdom means:

> ⁴ There are different kinds of gifts, but the same Spirit distributes them. ⁵ There are different kinds of service, but the same Lord. ⁶ There are different kinds of working, but in all of them and in everyone it is the same God at work. ⁷ Now to each one the manifestation of the Spirit is given for the common good. (1 Cor 12:4-7)

Scripture sets a clear expectation regarding growth in our Spirit-empowered kingdom lives. We are expected to "grow up" and "mature" in our faith. In fact, the gifts of the Spirit are given for this very purpose:

> ¹¹ So Christ himself gave the apostles, the prophets, the evangelists, the pastors and teachers, ¹² to equip his people for works of service, so that the body of Christ may be built up ¹³ until we all reach unity in the faith and in the knowledge of the Son of God and become mature, attaining to the whole measure of the

fullness of Christ. ¹⁴ Then we will no longer be infants, tossed back and forth by the waves, and blown here and there by every wind of teaching and by the cunning and craftiness of people in their deceitful scheming. ¹⁵ Instead, speaking the truth in love, we will grow to become in every respect the mature body of him who is the head, that is, Christ. (Eph 4:11-15)

The Means to Vibrant Faith

So scripturally speaking, a vibrant faith, while grounded in "sound teaching," is a personal trust in Jesus Christ which, empowered by the Holy Spirit, enthusiastically wells up into acts of faith, growing and maturing as it impels us to participate with God's people for his kingdom purposes. How is such vibrant faith to be nurtured and sustained?

According to the New Testament, Jesus is not only the one in whom we have faith but, in his own relationship with his Father, the very best exemplar of the means to achieve such vibrant faith. From his youth, he sought insight and understanding from God's word to Israel (Luke 2:46-49). He charted his kingdom course by what Scripture foretold about him (Luke 4:21; Matt 9:6; Matt 22:41-46). He took his kingdom manifesto from its pages (Luke 4:18-19). And he learnt the nature of kingdom power as he fed upon its truth (Matt 4:4; 20:18-19; Isa 53). Then, in communion with the Holy Spirit, as he lived and ministered out of this truth, he brought everything to his Father in prayer. It is a given that as a fully observant Jew, Jesus would have treasured and kept the usual rhythms and patterns of set prayers, corporate and personal, throughout his life,[8] but he also constantly sought quiet and solitude for his Father's company, comfort and wisdom (Mark 1:35-39; Luke 5:16; 6:12; 9:18-20). It was the quality of this life of prayer which caused his disciples to ask, "Lord, teach us to pray" (Luke 11:1).

N.T. Wright suggests that "When Jesus gave his disciples this prayer, he was giving them part of his own breath, his own life, his own prayer."[9] Clause by clause, they were invited into Jesus' own intimate relationship with his Father. They were called to worship as he did, and to invoke their Father's kingdom rule and authority, here and now, "as it is in heaven." On this basis, they were to call upon his provision for their daily bread, his empowerment for a life lived in the fullness of his grace, and his protection in temptation and trial – and all within the community of faith gathered in the name of "Our Father."

This kingdom community was also the place to share stories of faith – of the joys and challenges – which arose from participating in the life and labour of the kingdom:

> [7] Calling the Twelve to him, he began to send them out two by two and gave them authority over impure spirits. [30] The apostles gathered around Jesus and reported to him all they had done and taught. [31] Then, because so many people were coming and going that they did not even have a chance to eat, he said to them, "Come with me by yourselves to a quiet place and get some rest." [32] So they went away by themselves in a boat to a solitary place. (Mark 6:7, 30-32)

Sharing such stories, Jesus' followers were indeed to encourage and spur one another on, adding further fuel to their vibrant faith. Imagine the Marys returning from the empty tomb and keeping their news to themselves (Matt 28:1-10). Imagine Paul refusing to exhort the Ephesians or share his anguish with the Corinthians (2 Cor 12:1-10). Imagine John becoming tight-lipped about God's revelation (Rev 1:1-2). With every story, faith was stirred up and the vibrant cycle of devotion and kingdom participation refuelled.

Each of these elements of vibrant faith was taken up by following generations of believers. The "Church Fathers" taught that Christians should read a portion of the Bible every day and spend time in quiet meditation.[10] The Lord's Prayer and the Psalms were constant resources for prayer,[11] and even in the midst of the medieval professionalisation of spiritual practices, men and women of means continued to prioritise their own devotional lives, praying "the hours" and reading the stories of the lives of the saints.[12]

The role of prayer and Bible reading in vibrant faith was reemphasised by the Reformation. John Grayston argues:

> With the Reformation emphasis on the private interpretation of Scripture, the wider availability of printed Bibles and increasing standards of literacy the way was open for the development of the patterns of personal spirituality.[13]

Wesley's class system emphasized personal prayer and Bible reading as well alongside their communal reflections. Charles Simeon, one of the founding fathers of evangelicalism, reportedly rose every morning at four o'clock, and, after lighting his fire, devoted the first four hours of the day to private prayer and the devotional study of the Scriptures. These were the foundations of the so-called "Quiet Time," which reached its height of popularity in the twentieth century.[14] Scripture Union, which was founded in 1879, promoted a daily quiet time commencing with prayer, reading a daily text, examining and applying the text with the aid of questions and concluding with prayer. New Christians were thus encouraged to form the habit of this regular quiet time with God, a habit encouraged to the current day.

Reflection questions 5.2
1) What do you think is the most important insight regarding vibrant faith emerging from this survey of Scripture and tradition?

2) What does this survey of Scripture and tradition tell you about vibrant faith in *your* church?

Step Three: Wisdom

A Culture of Vibrant Faith

A vibrant faith in God, nurtured through prayer, Bible reading and the day-to-day experience of participating in his kingdom, can be a largely private activity. But, as we've seen, there are communal aspects to every element of such faith: the local church certainly has a role to play in nurturing and sustaining the vibrant faith its congregants. Organisational psychologists have persuasively demonstrated the power of organisational culture to shape human behaviour.[15] All organisations, including churches, have cultures. The question is whether or not they good and helpful cultures. If you sense that a church is "prayerless" for example, it can be useful to see this as a cultural issue. Similarly, if a church is observed to be "prayerful" this is a positive feature of the organisational culture. When it comes to fostering vibrant faith, organisational culture can be a powerful tool. If we can create a church culture where Bible reading, prayer and sharing stories about faith are highly valued, we can expect that current and future congregants will generally read the Bible, pray and share stories of faith more.

So, how do we change church culture so that it nurtures and sustains vibrant faith? In their classic paper on changing organisational culture, Silverzweig and Allen,[16] identify the critical influences on organisational culture that have been adapted here for church cultures:

- Leadership modelling behaviour: Behaviour is affected not just by what leaders pay lip service to, nor even what they actually do, but rather what leaders are *perceived* to be doing — by what *appears* to get their attention and priority.
- Ministry team and a small group culture: Most congregants are part of ministry teams or small groups which have specific sub-cultures of their own. This subculture is formed, reinforced and modified in the informal gatherings of the ministry team or small group. Hence leaders need to be involved in helping these ministry teams or small group develop a positive culture.
- Information and communication systems: The type of information, and the way it is communicated, has a powerful impact on culture and behaviour.
- Performance and reward systems: Cultures and behaviour are influenced by what is rewarded and recognised.
- Policies, structures and budgets: Policies, structures and budgets convey messages about cultural priorities. Procedures should support the agreed-upon culture, not undermine it.
- Training and orientation: New members of a congregation are open to understanding and complying with organisational culture if they are made aware of it.
- Results orientation: It is necessary to state specific, measurable objectives regarding the goals of culture change, and to monitor progress and provide regular feedback to the congregation on that progress.

We will look at how to apply this wisdom about shaping organisational culture in the Orthopraxy section of this chapter. But there are other factors related to vibrant faith that we also need to consider.

The Impact of Digitisation

The digital revolution has had, and will continue to have, an impact on the way that prayer, Bible reading and the sharing of faith stories occurs in Australia. We have witnessed the fourth major shift in the material form of the Bible: from scrolls to codices to printed books to digital formats.[17] Although print versions of the Bible remain top sellers, digital versions of the Bible are proliferating. YouVersion, a free mobile app created by the American megachurch Life.Church, has been installed on over 500 million devices worldwide. YouVersion also offers hundreds of reading plans with automated notifications which you can work through with your friends, to encourage frequent reading. Commercial software designed for the smart phone, tablet or desktop, such as Logos and GloBible, offer rich resources for Bible reading, while long-running websites like Bible Gateway offer quick free access to different translations.

This means that younger people in your church are more likely to read the Scriptures through their smart phone than as a printed Bible and the technology may actually be enhancing their reading. Van Peursen points out that "The printed book, containing the Bible from cover to cover... was just a phase in the history of the Bible... The Bible started without covers, so why should we worry about losing them again?"[18]

However, there are also concerns. Van Peursen points out:[19]

- A shift in textual medium may change human capacities and habits
- The meaning of a text is not independent from its formal presentation
- Digital reading encourages scanning, rather than close attention
- Digital devices encourage distraction.

When members of the congregation are asked to hold up their Bibles, many will now hold up their mobile phone. A printed Bible is always "just" a Bible and a permanent physical object. However, a mobile phone can be used for whole variety of purposes and when the app is closed the Bible "disappears." This material change can have an impact on the way that Christians read Bibles. There is also evidence that we retain more information when we read it from a printed page than we do from a screen.[20] Digital Bibles have "liquefied" the Bible through providing easy access to multiple translations, but this may undermine confidence in the text. The digitisation of the Bible also means that it has become more fragmented as the text can be presented independent of its context, and even more so as it is moved into social media. Churches need to think through these potential benefits and problems associated with digital Bibles. It is unlikely the trend can be reversed so we need to manage it thoughtfully.

The Importance of Story

As mentioned in the section on Scripture and tradition, the sharing of faith stories in the church community is a crucial part of vibrant faith. Although there are parts of the Bible, like the epistles, wisdom and the law, that are "propositional," most of the Scriptures are stories which convey a theological truth. Although we might be tempted to downplay the importance of stories in teaching theology, God's preference for using stories to transform people is clear in the Bible and confirmed by social science. The biblical stories, and the stories we tell one another, engage us at a deeper level than just intellectual propositions.[21]

> If faith were primarily an idea, the intellect alone might be adequate for dealing with it. Since it is instead a life to be lived, we need story. Story, as does life, engages all of what we are—mind, emotions, spirit, body. Faith calls us to live in a certain way, not just to think in a certain way.[22]

So one of the crucial things that we can do to grow faith in our congregations is to intentionally tell faith-building stories. One place we do this is when people give their "testimony." They are great examples of faith stories. But what about faith stories coming from day-to-day living in the midst of the unfolding of God's kingdom? Where do these stories get shared in your church? It is easy to convey faith building-stories in places like small groups or one-on-one conversations. This is more difficult in larger church gatherings. But if we cannot connect with the inspiring, faith-growing stories that are occurring across our churches, we are left impoverished.

Reflection questions 5.3
1) What does this survey of human wisdom tell you about growing faith?

2) What does this survey of human wisdom tell you about growing faith in *your* church?

Step 4: Orthopraxy

Our survey of Scripture, church history and wisdom has highlighted the interrelatedness of Bible reading, prayer and sharing stories of faith as our vibrant faith overflows into participating in God's kingdom work. We noted that even though Bible reading and prayer can be largely private practices, the church has an important role to play in fostering vibrant faith, and benefits directly from it. In particular, the church has an important role in:

- Supporting congregants in their devotional reading of the Bible including managing the digitisation of the Bible
- Helping congregants develop a vibrant prayer life
- Creating spaces for people to tell stories about the joys and challenges of their vibrant faith as it overflows into the life and work of the kingdom.

We have also identified that the best way to understand the prevalence, or lack of, prayer, devotional Bible reading and the sharing of faith-building stories in the life of the church is through the idea of church culture. If a church has a strong culture of prayer, Bible reading and sharing faith stories, its congregants are far more likely to be engaging in those practices and experiencing God in their life. Here we use the model of Silverzweig and Allen to make some suggestions of how you can make the culture of your church more conducive to vibrant faith.

1) Leadership modelling behaviour. The example of church leadership (you) is crucial in transforming organisational culture. If you want your church to have a culture of growing faith you need to *be seen* to be prayerful, engaging in personal Bible reading, experiencing the kingdom of God in your day-to-day life, and sharing faith-building stories. This presents a potential problem because we do not want to appear to be boastful. But if people do not see these things in their leaders they are unlikely to pursue them. So be self-aware of the danger here, but share what you are doing to ensure that your faith is vibrant. Take every opportunity to pray, don't just talk about

praying. When someone shares a prayer need, pray there and then. This not only makes sure you will not forget, but models prayerfulness. Share what God has been saying to you through your devotional reading. Share how God has been at work in your day-to-day life.

2) Ministry team and small group culture: Because you are one step removed from what happens in these subcultures you need to work hard at ensuring that the leaders of these ministry teams and small groups also value prayer, Bible reading, and sharing faith stories. Spend time sharing your passion for these things and create accountability structures whereby the ministry team and small group leaders can report on their support of these values. If you don't make it clear that prayer, Bible reading and sharing faith stories are really important, it can easily slip down the list of priorities for these ministry team and small group leaders.

3) Information and communication systems: As church leaders you need to be persistently highlighting the importance of prayer, Bible reading and awareness of God in day-to-day life. Preach on these things regularly. But you also need to create the channels for the faith-building stories to be shared throughout the entire church. People can always share faith stories in small groups, but can they share them with the whole church? There are no doubt great stories of God at work in people's lives in your church, but if the information cannot be passed through the community its potential to encourage others to grow in faith will be reduced. Create a culture where it is natural to share stories of what God is doing in your life with other people.

4) Performance and reward systems: You probably cannot provide people with financial rewards for their efforts related to prayer, Bible reading and sharing faith stories! But you can publicly celebrate these things as an encouragement for others. Publicly acknowledge the key role of pray-ers in the life of the church,

not just the do-ers. Acknowledge those who are committing themselves to daily Bible reading. Celebrate those who are courageous enough to share their faith-building stories.

5) Policies, structures and budgets: Create the structures whereby prayer, Bible reading, awareness of God in day-to-day life and the sharing of faith-building stories are "built in" to day-to-day functioning of the church. For example, make it a policy that every meeting in the church begins with people sharing stories of where they have experienced God in their lives since the last time they met. This might be challenging for some people, but it has the potential to transform the culture of your church. If people *are* actually growing in faith it will be easy to do! Engage in special seasons of prayer throughout the year e.g. Night of prayer, Three days of prayer, 40 days of prayer, 24/7 prayer. You might also consider having budget items related to prayer, Bible reading, awareness of God in everyday life and growing faith. Produce an annual "Thanksgiving booklet" filled with faith building stories contributed by congregants. It might be worth exploring the possibility of integrating the sermons with small group Bible studies and personal daily devotions, at least for a period in each year, if not most of the year.

6) Training and orientation: Provide plenty of training related to prayer, devotional Bible reading and seeing God in everyday life. Variety in prayer and Bible reading will help maintain enthusiasm. Ensure that all leaders are aware of the importance of these values. And make a special effort in orientation classes for new congregants to make them aware that prayer, Bible reading and seeing God in day-to-day life are a feature of your church culture.

7) Results orientation: Churches most likely to make progress in this area will fearlessly engage in trying to measure what is so crucial. For example, they may ask members of the church to anonymously identify how regularly they practice a daily devotional reading of the Bible and look for growing numbers

from year to year. They might also measure the attendance at prayer meetings, or how many faith-building stories are shared in Sunday services. At the very least you can monitor the "Alive and Growing Faith" core quality in your NCLS survey over the five year period.

Reflection questions 5.4
1) What do you feel is the most important insight regarding vibrant faith generated by this chapter?

2) Is there anything you are unsure of or disagree with?

3) What do you feel is the most important insight on growing vibrant faith *for your church* generated by this chapter?

4) What else could you do to foster vibrant faith in your church?

Step 5: Action
Here is a process which you might like to use or adapt for your context:

1) Gather together as a leadership and pray for the discernment of God's wisdom for your church with respect to growing faith.

2) Share together your answers to Reflection Questions 5.4.

3) Individually, write down your answer to the following question: What should our church *do* to foster growing faith? You might come up with up to five suggestions. Try to make your suggestions as specific as possible. For example, rather than just saying "Help people have vibrant faith," you could suggest something like "Integrate the sermons with small group studies and personal devotions for the first term of every year to promote personal bible reading and prayer," or "Have someone share a faith story at church each week."

4) Go around the group and have each member suggest one action the church could take to foster growing faith in your church.

Write the suggestion on a whiteboard or similar media. If your suggestion has already been made put a tick next to it on the whiteboard and then share your next suggestion.

5) When everyone has shared all of their suggestions, each member in the group is allocated three votes. (You might like to allocate each member three self-adhesive dots for this activity.) Each member can then use their votes. They can allocate all three votes to the same suggestion or utilise them across a number of suggestions.

6) Tally up the dots and you will have an indication of what, as a leadership team, might be a good action step to take to develop passionate spirituality in your church. Pray again and then decide which action steps you wish to take. Two or three is probably all that you can attempt at one time. Still, keep a record of your suggestions because you may be able to come back to them next year.

Conclusion

Christ's words to the church at Laodicea should make every church leadership team pause for serious thought. It is possible for a church to appear healthy, but if the faith of the congregation is lukewarm — lacking enthusiasm, failing to grow and thrive — it is literally a bad taste in the mouth of Jesus. As we have seen, the vibrant form of faith modelled by Jesus is his clear expectation for his church. Such faith cannot be pinned down to any single belief or spiritual practice, but rather thrives on the dynamic cycle of devotion through Bible reading and prayer, deepening our trust in Christ, which then overflows into the acts of faith which constitute our participation in the life and labour of the kingdom. As we share our stories of faith about the joys and challenges of this, our faith is increased further, and our devotion deepened. The result is an undeniably vibrant form of faith. The responsibility for some aspects of this certainly rests on the shoulders of individual members of our congregations but, as we have seen, church leadership teams have a vital role to play in building their church culture to support and encourage the practices of Bible-reading, prayer and sharing stories of faith. These are the crucial activities we need to seek to build into the culture of kingdom shaped churches. But they won't happen by themselves. We are engaged in a spiritual war, and a tactic of the enemy is to make us comfortable and apathetic. Our response is intentional and prayerful persistence.

Chapter Endnotes

1. Christian A. Schwarz, *Natural Church Development: A Guide to Eight Essential Qualities of Healthy Churches* (7th Updated and Revised Edition) (St. Charles: Churchsmart Resources, 2006).

2. Ruth Powell et al., *Enriching Church Life*, 2nd ed. (Saint Mary's: Mirrabooka Press & NCLS Research, 2012), 19.

3. See Appendix 2 for a fuller explanation of this.

4. Walter Brueggemann, *Reverberations of Faith: A Theological Handbook of Old Testament Themes* (Louisville: Westminster John Knox Press, 2002), 78.

5. Leon Morris, "Faith," in *New Bible Dictionary*, ed. D. R. W. Wood A. R. Millard, Donald J. Wiseman, I. Howard Marshall, J. I. Packer (Leicester: InterVarsity Press, 1996).

6. William F. Arndt, Frederick W. Danker, and Walter Bauer, *A Greek-English Lexicon of the New Testament and Other Early Christian Literature*, 3rd ed. (Chicago: University of Chicago Press, 2000), 426.

7. Bruce A Demarest, "Introduction," in *Four Views on Christian Spirituality* ed. Bruce A. Demarest (Grand Rapids: Zondervan Academic, 2012), 17.

8. I. Howard Marshall, "Jesus – Example and Teacher of Prayer in the Synoptic Gospels," in *Into God's Presence: Prayer in the New Testament*, ed. Richard N. Longenecker (Cambridge: Wm. B. Eerdmans, 2001), 116.

9. Tom Wright, *The Lord and His Prayer* (London: SPCK Publishing, 2012), 2.

10 Adolph Harnack, *New Testament Studies* (London: Williams, 1907-1925), Vol. 5, 125.

11 Andrew B. McGowan, *Ancient Christian Worship: Early Church Practices in Social, Historical, and Theological Perspective* (Grand Rapids: Baker Academic, 2014), 187; Joseph A. Jungmann, *Christian Prayer through the Centuries* (Mahwah: Paulist Press, 2007), 17.

12 Jungmann, *Christian Prayer*, 78.

13 John Grayston, "The Bible and Spirituality: The Decline in Biblical Literacy among Evangelicals and the Future of the Quiet Time," *ANVIL* 19, no. 2 (2002).

14 Ibid., 104.

15 See for example Edgar H. Schein, *Organizational Culture and Leadership* (San Francisco: Jossey Bass, 1985).

16 Stan Silverzweig and Robert F. Allen, "Changing the Corporate Culture," *Sloan Management Review* 17, no. 3 (1976).

17 Jeffrey S. Siker, *Liquid Scripture: The Bible in a Digital World* (Minneapolis: Fortress Press, 2017), 2.

18 Wido van Peursen, "Is the Bible Losing Its Covers? Conceptualization and Use of the Bible on the Threshold of the Digital Order," *Hiphil Novum* 1, no. 1 (2014): 57.

19 Ibid., 58.

20 Siker, 4.

21 Daniel Taylor, "Story-Shaped Faith," in *The Power of Words and the Wonder of God*, ed. John Piper and Justin Taylor (Wheaton: Crossway Books, 2009).

22 Ibid., 106.

Chapter 6
Inspiring Worship

Introduction

Worship is the inevitable response to the revelation of God in all his sovereign glory. There will come a time when, "All the nations you have made shall come and bow down before you, O Lord, and shall glorify your name" (Ps 86:9) but, here and now, such worship is distinctively the Church's great privilege and responsibility.

From beginning to end, the purpose of this worship is... worship: to behold God faithfully and respond fittingly so that God is pleased and glorified. Then, and only then, may we judge worship by how it impacts us. But impact us it must, inspiring us so that we may indeed worship wholeheartedly and be re-formed to serve God's kingdom purposes until Christ comes again. As we behold our King, we become kingdom people who together proclaim, embody and enact God's kingdom reign.

We need to recognise, of course, that "worship" certainly has meaning beyond the gathered church services in view in this chapter. Worship is an attitude that we're called to take across every facet of our lives, expressed through personal devotion to God and acts of service which reflect God's nature, both within and beyond the community of faith. Yet, as we'll explore in this chapter, our corporate worship plays a vital role in our lives together.

The research indicates that vital churches have engaging, Christ-exalting, passionate, vital, nurturing and meaningful worship.[1] We think the word "inspiring" is a good summary of these descriptions. The word inspiration comes from the Latin *inspirare* meaning to "blow into, breathe upon," or figuratively speaking to excite or inflame. This phenomenon is vital to our times of gathered worship as we come together to behold our God and King and God breathes fresh and invigorating life into us.

In these terms, the act of corporate or gathered worship is a high calling and a privilege which should delight God's people. Yet, this idea seems hard to reconcile with the "worship wars" which have been waged in many of our churches over recent decades. Those in church leadership often bear the brunt of the steady flow of complaints which seem to flow in place of the awe and wonder the Bible's vision expresses. The message is too long or too short. There are too few or too many hymns/songs, too much or too little volume, too much or too little structure... Bible reading... freedom in the Spirit... time for the children. What we can take from this is that our corporate worship is of great concern to at least some of those who attend our churches!

However, the NCLS data indicate that a large majority of attenders "always or usually" find inspiration, a sense of God's presence, growth in understanding their faith, music they appreciate, and helpful preaching, through their participation in corporate worship.[2] Further, the NCD research shows that inspiring worship has less to do with the form of worship (i.e., liturgical, traditional, contemporary) than the inspirational quality of the service itself.[3] The crucial thing is that people in vital churches attend church not out of duty but because they experience the inbreaking of the kingdom of God in their worship services, whether that be through singing, sermon, liturgy, sacraments, fellowship or something else.

The significance of corporate worship may have been tested through the shutdowns forced by the Covid-19 crisis of 2020-2022, but, as we explore below, both Scripture and wisdom attest to the centrality of inspiring worship to our sense of what it means to be "church."

Step One: Context

Our task in this section, as always, is to think through our current context; the what, the how and the why of corporate or gathered worship in the churches we lead. In our next two sections we will look at the resources which point us to what could or should be happening in our worship, but before we get to these, we need to take a clear-sighted look at what's already at work. It will be important therefore to remember that there are many aspects that fall outside the imperatives or "should-ness" of worship. As we'll explore further below, Christian churches have developed a rich array of forms of worship, and individuals may be drawn to, or simply accustomed to, a specific expression of worship. What we grow up with will greatly influence what we prefer, but so too will our personalities, peak or transformative experiences, and our cultural background. We need, therefore, to guard against confusing matters of taste or custom with the imperatives of worship. So, for the moment, set aside your foredrawn conclusions and let's explore.

Reflection questions 6.1

1) One of the NCLS core qualities that your church survey would measure is "Vital and Nurturing Worship." How does your church rate on this measure? What are your reflections on this?

2) What are the key values of your church when it comes to corporate worship?

Step Two: Scripture and Tradition

As we have discussed in earlier chapters, one of the major themes of the Bible is the kingdom of God. Since the fall when humans sought to deny the sovereignty of God, God has been pursuing an agenda to restore God's righteous kingdom on earth. Beginning with Abraham and the nation of Israel we see God's plan unfolding. As we have seen it reached its climax with the life and ministry of Jesus:

> [14] After John was put in prison, Jesus went into Galilee, proclaiming the good news of God. [15] "The time has come," he said. "The kingdom of God has come near. Repent and believe the good news!" (Mark 1:14-15)

However, even though the kingdom has arrived, it has not been fulfilled. The kingdom (reign) of God is clearly observable at certain times in certain places, but we need no convincing that human sin and evil are still powerful forces at work in our world. So we live with an awareness of the kingdom of God on earth as "now and not yet." In our personal lives, families and communities we see the promising green shoots of the kingdom but we long for its perfection and consummation in our world.

And the "now and not yet" scenario plays out in our church lives as well. Through the power of the Holy Spirit your local church is joining with God in the unrolling of his kingdom but at the same time finds itself living with the realities of sin and suffering. It is therefore vital in our corporate worship that we find the inspiration to continue our kingdom labour. Although our worship also experiences the tension of the now and not yet, it promises us a taste of what the consummation of the kingdom will look like.

The hope of the great kingdom banquet appears throughout the biblical narrative (see Ex 12, Num 9, Esth 9, Isa 25:6, Luke 14:15, Rev 19:7-9). The people of God are encouraged to eat and celebrate together the salvation from God as they look forward to joining the great heavenly banquet. And this is one of the purposes of our corporate worship – to have a foretaste of the coming of the kingdom of God. As Peterson writes:

> This hope of what will be empowers the church not to seek escape from this life but to participate by and with the Spirit to embody more fully the kingdom of God on earth as it is in heaven... communal worship is the church's primary activity whereby God inspires, empowers, and sends the gathered for such an end.[4]

Our local church worship may be far from perfect. The singing might be out of key, the preaching might go too long, the fellowship might be a little shallow, but it is in the gathering of the local church that the people of God gather to experience the kingdom of God and pray for its consummation. And so this chapter focuses on how we can make our local church gatherings an even better foretaste of the great kingdom banquet in heaven and which we hope to see established here on earth.

The worship practices of the earliest churches are strongly suggestive of what the worship in your local church should look like:

> They devoted themselves to the apostles' teaching and to fellowship, to the breaking of bread and to prayer (Acts 2:42).

Preaching the Word of God, fellowship (or perhaps more helpfully, "partnership"), the breaking of bread and prayer are therefore fundamental elements of local church worship. But beyond these we believe two adjectives (authentic and participatory) emerge from both the Old and New Testaments that we would encourage you to reflect on as you consider the corporate worship at your local church.

Authentic

God not only reveals himself in Scripture but also provides through it a record of how God has inspired people to respond authentically in worship. Under the kingdom treaty with Israel, God provided the word (the law and the prophets which recounted his character and dealings with Israel) and the tabernacle/temple (in which they encountered God's sovereign presence) as deep wells of revelation for their worship. Then, with its sacrifices and feasts, the temple served as the focus for Israel's response to her divine king: from God's fearsome holiness marked by the Day of Atonement to God's mighty works of salvation commemorated at Passover, and God's ongoing provision for them celebrated in the Feast of Weeks, God's people remembered and celebrated the kaleidoscope of God's royal nature and sovereign care for them in their worship.

The New Testament church also practised a range of authentic worshipful responses to the revelation of God through Christ. The early churches, and many through history, focussed on the public reading of Scripture, and teaching and exhortation from it:

> [13] Until I come, devote yourself to the public reading of Scripture, to preaching and to teaching. (1 Tim 4:13)

In response, worshippers participated by confessing their faith, and fragments of such "creeds" or "confessions" can be found at various places in the New Testament. The epistles are full of what Ross Allen summarises as "doxologies, benedictions, and invocations of praise," such as Ephesians 1:3-15, which, even in the midst of praise, teach and ground believers' faith in the Trinity, all "to the praise of his glory."[5] Singing included the use of psalms (certainly including, but not limited to, the Old Testament Psalter); hymns (such as "The Magnificat" in Luke 1:46-55 and Phil 2:6-11); and "spiritual songs" which welled up as a result of the work of the Holy Spirit (1 Cor 14:26). But, equally, corporate prayer was also central to early forms of communal worship. According to Acts, believers met regularly for prayer (Acts 2:42), praying for guidance (1:24), preservation from trouble (4:24-30), deliverance from persecution (12:5, 12), and wisdom in ministry (13:1-3; 14:23). The confession of sin and the reception of forgiveness were also seen as vital responses to God's self-revelation as both holy and forgiving (Matt 4:48; 1 John 1:9; Jas 5:16). Some point to the importance of corporate lament in the life of ancient Israel and suggest it has an important part to play in contemporary local church worship.[6]

The Lord's supper, communion or Eucharist has a particularly important part to play corporate worship. It provides a bridge between our current reality and the heavenly kingdom banquet that is taking place at this very moment. Paul highlighted this when he said, "Whenever you eat this bread and drink this cup, you proclaim the Lord's death until he comes" (1 Cor 11:26). Certainly, the Lord's supper should be a sombre event, but it is also sometimes a joyful event, not in a superficial manner, but as a deep experience of Christian hope.

Such a discussion highlights the incredible diversity of activities that went on in the early churches and prompts questions like these: How varied and authentic are our worship services? If we were to list all of the elements we use in our service, how long or short would that this be?

In some traditions the worship services can be quite "boisterous" with lots of singing, shouting and physical involvement. Other traditions are more comfortable with "quieter" worship. However, all Christian life, including gathered worship, should be marked by diverse and authentic responses to the revelation of God. Sometimes the revelation of God will bring celebration. But at other times it will bring confession. Sometimes joy. Sometimes lament. Sometimes thanksgiving. Sometimes petition. Sometimes intimacy. Sometimes reverent awe. Sometimes singing. Sometimes silence. Whatever activity of corporate worship is being undertaken it should be an authentic response to the revelation of God, not habit. Our corporate worship services are sometimes prone to become fairly monochromatic and predictable. Shaped by tradition we sometimes heavily emphasise one aspect of worship (singing, liturgy, lament, joy, reverence etc) and fail to authentically respond to the diverse revelation of God. Changing the traditional worship style of a church, whether that be word-focused, singing-focused, liturgy-focused or some other focus, is a difficult thing. But we think the biblical and church historical discussion above should at least cause us to reflect on what types of diverse and authentic responses to the revelation of God might we be overlooking.

Participatory

The picture of kingdom worship we have in Scripture is also one of widespread participation. Paul's advice to the church in Corinth reveals to us some of the elements of corporate worship that featured in the earliest churches.

> [26] What then shall we say, brothers and sisters? When you come together, each of you has a hymn (lit. "song"), or a word of instruction, a revelation, a tongue or an interpretation. Everything must be done so that the church may be built up (1 Cor 14:26).

Participation in worship extended well beyond those who might lead such gatherings to include the whole congregation. Each and every one of them were to approach God's royal throne with "boldness," and to enter into the holy of holies "in full assurance of faith" through Jesus, their great high priest, to bring their worship and to minister to one another (Heb 10:19-25). Your church is meant to be a "*a polycentric-participative community*,"[7] orchestrated by the Holy Spirit where everyone participates in worship in some way.

Different Christian traditions will interpret this passage differently. Some churches, like the Brethren assemblies, would interpret it literally meaning that each member of the congregation should come with something to publicly share. Those from the Pentecostal tradition would emphasise the importance of spiritual gifts like speaking in tongues during worship. Others would emphasise the "word of instruction" from Paul's list. However, regardless of the tradition, we should consider the participatory nature of corporate worship that Paul is advocating. *Each of the church members is encouraged to participate in the worship in some way.* Worship should never be passive. Each member is to bring some ministry to corporate worship for the building up of others in the church.

Step Three: Wisdom

NCLS research has indicated that regardless of a church's tradition, the level of inspiration a person receives from a worship service is dependent on such factors as:

- A sense of God's presence
- Awe or mystery
- Joy
- Growth in understanding of God
- Preaching that is helpful to everyday life.[8]

According to Schwarz inspiring worship has less to do with the form of worship (i.e., liturgical, traditional, contemporary) than with the inspirational quality of the service itself.[9] The crucial thing is that people in vital churches attend church not out of duty but because they *experience* the living God at their worship services, whether this be through singing, the sermon, the liturgy, the sacraments or the fellowship. Each of these elements provides opportunity for God's self-revelation and provide the means to offer their worshipful response. As Stetzer and Rainer identify, this will often overflow into a sense of anticipation and expectation associated with worship in vital churches – the people at these churches expect God to do something in their gathered worship, and God usually does![10]

The choice and style of worship songs remains a contentious issue for many churches. However, research across the Western world confirms the conclusions of the NCLS:

> Churches that wish to connect better with younger people in their local communities should consider the issue of contemporary worship. While churches rightly question the place of popular culture in church life, when it comes to being attractive to potential joiners, churches that are more in tune with contemporary musical cultures tend to be more attractive.[11]

This is a difficult reality for many churches. You do not always need contemporary music in order to attract and hold younger people, but it does appear to be easier when this is the case. A conflict over worship styles will certainly do nothing to add to the vitality of your church. However, the decision to make 18th to 20th century music the focus of your worship services is one that churches should consciously make in the knowledge that it will make attracting younger people more difficult.

Interestingly, alongside this impetus to contemporary styles of worship music, research suggests that those whom Robert Webber terms "Younger Evangelicals"[12] may also be inclined to "re-appropriate ancient traditions as a way into the future."[13] In other words, at least some younger people are attracted to older and more formal styles of worship. In his wide-ranging research into *Evangelicals, Worship and Participation*, Alan Rathe suggests that such ancient traditions might offer some redress to the low levels of congregational participation he believes are prevalent in evangelical worship.[14]

Beyond its significance for worship itself, participation in corporate worship fosters a sense of community. Many of the elements of corporate worship are exactly those factors which the social sciences tell us contribute to a sense of belonging and community: sharing values and beliefs, connecting with others through words and actions, giving and receiving encouragement, and sharing stories about the past, present and future. Worshipping together fulfills a whole set of human needs, and whilst this is not the main aim of worship (worship is the main aim of worship!), it is a significant side-effect which encourages God's people and further strengthens them for their kingdom labours.

Such strengthening of the bonds of community is in itself formative. As the bonds of community are strengthened, we become more fully a gathering of God's kingdom people. Sociological insights bear out this (re)formative potential in worship. As philosopher, James K.A. Smith points out, there is something going on when we meet together to worship, week after week and year after year: we are indeed being *formed*.[15] As Smith has argued across his *Cultural Liturgies* series, we are mistaken if we think that as human persons we conduct our lives based solely on what we think and believe. Rather, he argues, we are shaped by our desires, which are, in turn, formed by those *repeated embodied acts* in which we engage across every context of our lives.[16] From our trips to the shopping centre to other immersive experiences such as cheering at the footy stadium or socialising at the backyard BBQ, each of these activities act at every level — social, physical, emotional, cognitive and ethical — to form us into particular types of people. And this, as Smith claims, is exactly the way in which Christian worship should also function, with the specific aim of countering the distortions of our secular activities which make us into individualistic spectators and consumers and forming us, instead, into the image of Christ our King. Every sight and sound, every movement and posture, every word and song, should reorientate us to the gospel of God's kingdom and the work of the Holy Spirit in our faith communities and our world.

Reflection questions 6.3
1) What does this survey of human wisdom tell you about church worship?

2) What does this survey of human wisdom tell you about *your* church's worship?

Step 4: Orthopraxy

No one form or style of worship can claim to be the guarantor of the adequacy of our worship. More formal forms of liturgy are always in danger of being learnt by rote rather than by heart. Free forms of worship are always in danger of neglecting theological clarity and depth. Formal liturgy may lack contextuality and space for the Spirit. Free forms of worship may neglect attention to the full range of Scripture and the elements of worship. Traditional or contemporary; formal or free; focused on head or heart or hands; word or table? Our besetting sins remain the confusion of matters of taste with matters of substance, and an inattention to the depth and breadth of God's design for our worship which begins, continues and ends in God.

For some churches the expectation will be that you meet God through the corporate worship and singing. For other churches your expectation is that you will meet God through the preaching of the word. For other churches the most powerful point of connection with God will be through the liturgy. For others, participation in the sacraments. For others, the movement of the Spirit. For all churches, the crucial question is, *where are we expecting to meet God and experience the kingdom in our worship services, and what are we doing to make sure that it happens?*

Our God and King revels in self-revelation to his people and it is God who initiates and enables our worship. Our first task, therefore, is to ensure that the structure and content of our times of gathered worship play their part in facilitating this. Through the word in Scripture and by the Holy Spirit, God desires that we intentionally enter God's presence and behold God, most especially in the person of the Son, Jesus Christ. Every aspect of God's character and every feature of saving work will require our attention in due course and the resources of the early and historical Church (such as liturgical formulations, the church calendar and the lectionary) may enable our churches to more broadly, deeply and authentically engage with God's diverse self-revelation.

Each facet of God's character and saving work should inspire some form of authentic worshipful response. These may range from adoration to repentance, commitment, assent, thanksgiving, lament or homage, but as is appropriate to our context and season, the whole range of kingdom experience should be encompassed in our times of gathered worship from time to time.

Participative worship should seek to involve every member of the congregation as much as possible so that, in our joint priesthood, our churches bring God the worship God is due. This also enables every member of the congregation to encounter God for themselves and for God to inspire them in their kingdom life and labour. There are many expressions of participation, ranging from the spontaneous to the liturgical, from the silent to the sung, spoken and enacted, but maximal engagement for every believer present should be our goal.

Our times of gathered worship should form, reform and transform our congregations into those living kingdom shaped lives in kingdom shaped churches. This may occur in a flash of revelation or over the much longer term as our worship activities, week by week, counter the influence of our individualistic and consumer culture. The communal and ethical implications of our worship may well require greater exploration and explanation, and this will in turn inspire deeper worship of the King whose kingdom is a realm of shared blessing and justice.

Reflection questions 6.4
1) What do you feel is the most important insight regarding inspiring corporate worship generated by this chapter?

2) Is there anything you are unsure of or disagree with?

3) What do you feel is the most important insight on inspiring corporate worship *for your church* generated by this chapter?

Step 5: Action

Few areas of church life insight as much passion as corporate worship. During your discussions of the material in this chapter you may have already experienced some differences of opinion. And so this is a topic we need to navigate with grace and care for one another. Please recognise that your passionately held beliefs about worship style may not be shared by others in the leadership or the church. And please remember that decisions about worship in your church are not ultimately about *you* but about pleasing God and the preferences of others:

> ³ Do nothing out of selfish ambition or vain conceit. Rather, in humility value others above yourselves, ⁴ not looking to your own interests but each of you to the interests of the others (Phil 2:3-4).

Here is a process which you might like to use or adapt to develop some action steps towards developing even more inspiring worship your church:

1) Gather together as a leadership and pray for the discernment of God's wisdom for your church with respect to your church worship.

2) Share together your answers to Reflection Questions 6.4.

3) Individually, write down your answer to the following question: What should we do, as leadership, to make our worship services even more inspiring? You might come up with up to five suggestions. Try to make your suggestions as specific as possible. For example, rather than just saying "Be more authentic," you could suggest something like "Set aside once a month for people in the worship service to worship God in a

way we don't normally," or "Identify two new components for inclusion in our worship services that promote participation."

4) Go around the group and have each member suggest one action the church could take to encourage even more inspiring corporate worship. Write the suggestion on a whiteboard or similar media. If your suggestion has already been made put a tick next to it on the whiteboard and then share your next suggestion.

5) When everyone has shared all of their suggestions, each member in the group is allocated three votes. (You might like to allocate each member three self-adhesive dots for this activity.) Each member can then use their votes. They can allocate all three votes to the same suggestion or utilise them across a number of suggestions.

6) Tally up the dots and you will have an indication of what, as a leadership team, might be a good action step to take to with respect to your corporate worship. Pray again and then decide which action steps you wish to take. Two or three is probably all that you can attempt at one time. Keep a record of your suggestions because you may be able to come back to them next year.

Conclusion

Worship begins and ends with God. It is only possible because, God lovingly chooses to self-reveal as our God and King. The term "ineffability" might have fallen out of common usage, but it captures God's manifold greatness and mystery which immeasurably exceed any human expression. In God's character and redeeming work in Jesus Christ, across all eternity we will never run out of reasons to fall prostrate in worship before the one seated on the throne (Rev 4:10). We do not need to be entertained, we need to worship, and in this we will find the abiding hope and joy which will sustain us.

To even begin to behold our King cannot fail to inspire us. This inspiration, through God's word in Scripture and by the Holy Spirit, enables our authentic response and forms and reforms us. As we participate together, we are transformed into "a royal priesthood, a holy nation, God's own people" (1 Pet 2:9) living kingdom shaped lives in kingdom shaped churches. Strangely, our corporate worship achieves this by, in a sense, paying us no attention at all. Our worship counters the deformative effects of our culture, acting as God's vaccine against our consumerism, our strident individualism, and our deep self-involvement by affirming that worship is not all about me; it's not even all about us; it is, in the end, all about God.

Chapter Endnotes

1. Ruth Powell et al., "Models of Church Vitality: A Literature Review," *NCLS Occasional Paper* 39 (2019).

2. Ruth Powell and Kathy Jacka, "Attenders Overall Experiences in Church Worship Services," National Church Life Survey, https://www.ncls.org.au/articles/attenders-overall-experiences-in-church-worship-services/.

3. Christian Schwarz, *Natural Church Development* (Emmelsbull: C. and P. Publishing, 1996), 31.

4. Brent D. Peterson, *Created to Worship: God's Invitation to Become Fully Human* (Kansas City: Beacon Hill Press, 2012), 54.

5. Allen P. Ross, *Recalling the Hope of Glory: Biblical Worship from the Garden to the New Creation* (Grand Rapids: Kregel Academic, 2006), 438.

6. Josh Lee, "Why Lament Is Important in Worship," The Gospel Coalition (Canada), https://ca.thegospelcoalition.org/article/why-lament-is-important-in-worship/.

7. Miroslav Volf, "Community Formation as an Image of the Triune God: A Congregational Model of Church Order and Life," in *Community Formation in the Early Church and in the Church Today*, ed. Richard N. Longenecker (Peabody: Hendrickson 2002), 231.

8. Ruth Powell et al., *Enriching Church Life*, 2nd ed. (Saint Marys: Mirrabooka Press & NCLS Research, 2012), 14.

9. Schwarz, 31.

10 Ed Stetzer and Thom S Rainer, *Transformational Church: Creating a New Scorecard for Congregations* (Nashville: B&H Publishing Group, 2010), 150.

11 Powell et al., 15.

12 Robert E. Webber, *The Younger Evangelicals: Facing the Challenges of the New World*, 10th Edition (Grand Rapids: Baker Publishing Group, 2002), 41.

13 Alan Rathe, *Evangelicals, Worship and Participation: Taking a Twenty-First Century Reading* (Burlington: Routledge, 2014), 13.

14 Rathe, 26.

15 James K. A. Smith, *Imagining the Kingdom: How Worship Works* (Grand Rapids: Baker Academic, 2013).

16 *You Are What You Love: The Spiritual Power of Habit* (Grand Rapids: Brazos, 2016).

Chapter 7
Intentional Discipleship

Introduction

Citizenship of the "kingdom" of Australia may be attained by one of two means. It is either received by virtue of being born in Australia to at least one Australian parent or acquired by application and the successful completion of a citizenship test. How like our God to ignore such rules. Our citizenship of God's kingdom is by *new* birth and is all gift:

> [13] But now in Christ Jesus you who once were far off have been brought near by the blood of Christ... [19] Consequently, you are no longer foreigners and strangers, but fellow citizens with God's people and also members of his household. (Eph 2:13, 19)

Yet, having been saved through Christ's sacrifice, and "brought near" in him, there stands before us a lifetime of discipleship – of growing into our citizenship of God's kingdom. As Dallas Willard expresses it:

> Spiritual formation and discipleship are all about development of the life in the kingdom of God that comes to us through the risen Christ. As a disciple of Jesus, I am living with Him, learning to live in the kingdom of God as He lived in the kingdom of God.[1]

What does this entail? For Australian citizenship, there's a booklet entitled "Our Common Bond,"[2] which sets out some history, demography, our "democratic beliefs, rights and liberties," and even attempts to summarise Australian values. If you apply to become an Australian, you'll need to pass a test on its contents. So, there are things you'll need to know before you "pass" but there are also ongoing expectations about what being a citizen will mean. There are things to do: you'll need, for example, to obey the law, vote in elections and defend Australia if needed. Then there are freedoms (of speech, association and religion) to uphold. And values (equality, tolerance and compassion) to respect. Those who become citizens commit themselves to all this through their pledge of allegiance.

As we've already seen, those who come to faith in Christ and pledge their allegiance to him, may be at different points along the way in the process of adopting the forms of belief and life which enact our heavenly citizenship. But the final product will always be what Paul calls maturity – the fullness of Christ:

> [11] So Christ himself gave the apostles, the prophets, the evangelists, the pastors and teachers, [12] to equip his people for works of service, so that the body of Christ may be built up [13] until we all reach unity in the faith and in the knowledge of the Son of God and become mature, attaining to the whole measure of the fullness of Christ. (Eph 4:11-13)

Jesus plays a dual role in this for us. He is both King of this now and not yet kingdom, *and* citizen *par excellence*. A look around our world teaches us that this is far from the usual state of affairs. All too often, those who rule over us behave as if the law of the land – legal or ethical – doesn't apply to them. So often they try to get away with what they can – but not Jesus, who instead perfectly fulfills his Father's law. Our worldly leaders' catchcry, explicit or not, is all too often, "Do as I say. Not as I do." But not our King. "Follow me," he says. "Watch me. Do as I do. Love as I love," he says. "Come and be my disciple."

We follow a king like no other for a kingdom like no other.

When the NCLS team did their meta-analysis of the empirical research into the features of vital churches, they did indeed identify that discipleship is a crucial quality.[3] However, the terms generated by the researchers relating to this quality were quite diverse, including transforming discipleship, maturation of believers, intentional faith development, learning and growing in community, and holistic small groups. In one sense, this diversity if hardly surprising. Discipleship – growing into our kingdom citizenship – entails every aspect of the Christian life. The key thing is that we be intentional – hence the title of this chapter. Our hope is to identify some key principles and methods which will enable you as a church leadership team to intentionally pursue discipleship for your church whatever your context.

Step 1: Context

Churches approach the task of discipleship in different ways depending upon their history, tradition and current church leadership. But often the way we go about growing disciples of Jesus Christ in our churches is assumed rather than intentionally pursued. We might assume that discipleship is going on, but if pressed we are not quite sure how or where it is happening.

There are a number of different ways that discipleship might be occurring in your church. Preaching, corporate worship, small-group Bible studies, mentoring relationships, Sunday school, vacation Bible schools, personal devotions, reading, listening to podcasts and watching videos are all places where discipleship can occur. But how is discipleship *actually happening* in your church?

Reflection questions 7.1

1) How is discipleship done in your church?

2) What evidence do you have that discipleship is occurring in your church? How do you measure discipleship?

3) Do you have any "formal" discipleship programs operating? How successful are they?

4) How do you go about helping parents to disciple their children?

Step 2: Scripture and Tradition

In first century Judaism travelling rabbis with disciples in a master-apprentice type relationship certainly weren't uncommon. These disciples usually approached the rabbi and asked to "follow him" physically and spiritually, so that over time they would become like that rabbi.[4] Although the ministry of Jesus was distinct (for example, Jesus called his disciples to follow him), in the Gospels we see Jesus was still acting very much like a rabbi discipling his followers.[5] As the disciples were "disciplined" they grew to resemble him. Jesus concluded, "Everyone who is fully trained will be like his teacher" (Luke 6:40). Although there was a small group of disciples called "the twelve," we also see reference to many other disciples of Jesus in the Gospels (e.g., Luke 6:17).

For those who were called by Jesus there was a choice to make. Although their allegiance to Jesus would grow as they came to understand his identity and mission, his summons to follow him demanded that they count the cost of placing everything — wealth, family, even life itself — in submission to their allegiance to him and his kingdom.[6] They were to commit themselves entirely to him, denying themselves and following him even to the cross:

> [24] Then Jesus said to his disciples, "Whoever wants to be my disciple must deny themselves and take up their cross and follow me. (Matt 16:24)

In return, Jesus offered none of the usual prestige and security associated with following a recognised rabbi (Luke 9:57-58). Rather, he offered his disciples his company, access to his teachings, and times of fellowship to explore and understand these. They observed firsthand his relationship with his Father in prayer and worship, and watched on as he dealt with everyone from the demanding crowds to his ever-present enemies. They saw him perform miracles and were drawn into the action of these. He revealed his identity and kingdom plans to them and commissioned them to participate in his kingdom mission. He was their messiah and saviour, but also their master, rabbi, example, mentor and friend. This was a deeply relational form discipleship.

The Great Commission

So, when at last the risen Jesus commissioned these disciples to "go" and "make disciples," they were well prepared:

> [18] Then Jesus came to them and said, "All authority in heaven and on earth has been given to me. [19] Therefore go and make disciples of all nations, baptizing them in the name of the Father and of the Son and of the Holy Spirit, [20] and teaching them to obey everything I have commanded you. And surely I am with you always, to the very end of the age." (Matt 28:18-20)

First, unlike other rabbis, we learn here that Jesus commissions his followers based on his own sovereign authority, received from the Father to fulfill every kingdom purpose: he is "the king in the present-and-coming kingdom of God, the one who represents God's cosmic rule."[7] On this basis, Jesus now in turn power-fully authorizes his disciples to take the gospel of this kingdom to all nations. In Chapter 3, we saw that this "going" was not only geographical (though it certainly was this) but a call to make discipleship a part of their everyday coming and going. As they won new believers, they were to declare them God's own through baptism, under the seal of the triune name,[8] implying their dedication, submission and belonging.[9] And, of course, they were to train these new believers in "all that I have commanded you," so that all his disciples might obey Jesus in everything, submitting to the gospel of his kingdom reign.

All this was to take place in the context of Jesus' continuing presence. His ongoing presence *with them* and even *in them* by his Holy Spirit after his ascension, would mean that each new believer became a disciple, not of those who carried out this delegated discipleship, but of Jesus Christ himself.[10] Rather than diminishing the significance of their disciple-making, this reality heightened the importance of what they did and shaped how Jesus' first disciples went about their task of fulfilling his Great Commission.

The Apostolic Church

The remainder of the New Testament may therefore be read as an account of this discipleship undertaking and how the local church played its part in it. Michael Wilkins points out that in Acts Luke consistently uses "disciples" to designate believers.[11] Discipleship was intrinsic to belief, not an optional extra for a small elite. Such discipleship was unmediated in that, by the Holy Spirit, Jesus himself did indeed continue to disciple each and every believer himself. Nevertheless, he called upon his body, the Church, to be physically, relationally and spiritually present in order to carry out the "communal enterprise" of discipleship.[12]

This communal discipleship operated at three levels. Firstly, the gathered church provided the context in which teaching and formation occurred through God's word and by his Spirit, in its preaching, teaching and worship. The Apostles' teaching was central to this, relating Jesus' life and ministry and all that he had taught them. At a second level, as believers met for fellowship in household and small group contexts, there was opportunity to share further teaching and stories of faith, and to reflect on the encouragement and challenges of living out their discipleship.[13] Thirdly, those among the church community whose lives demonstrated maturity in discipleship, spent time, one to one, with others seeking to minister out of their own discipleship under Christ to make disciples of others.[14]

And Beyond

In the following two thousand years, the Church has emphasised various terms and methods drawn from Scripture for its discipleship practices.

For the gathered church, for example, preaching has retained its importance across the intellectual, ethical and devotional domains of discipleship. C.H. Spurgeon, the nineteenth century "Prince of Preachers," preached a winsome form of Calvinist orthodoxy and passionately exhorted his listeners to discipleship characterised by "wholeheartedness," "continuance," "brotherly love," and "fruit bearing."[15] Preaching God's word has always been, and remains, a highly significant "means of calling people to discipleship and teaching them its implications."[16]

But preaching is not the only tool of discipleship. Jesus discipled his followers in small groups (for example, Mark 10:42). In Luke 10 and Matthew 10 we see Jesus using "learning by doing" to disciple his followers. He sent them out in pairs to do what he had been teaching and demonstrating to them, and when the disciples returned they reflected on their experience together. Priscilla and Aquila discipled Apollos in his home (Acts 18:26). Paul mentored Timothy and Titus remotely — the pastoral epistles are an early example of distance learning!

Small groups meeting in homes have been a widely used and effective method of discipleship through much of the history of the church. This is not surprising because Paul's conceptualization of church as "family" was a significant metaphor for the church.[17] The small gatherings of the early churches were not just dictated by availability but a theological conviction that a home is an important venue for discipleship.

Another reason that small groups are important is because discipleship depends so heavily on imitation (1 Cor. 11:1). And imitation requires interpersonal contact in a variety of life contexts, many of which are not possible in a larger group.

Another theological driver for discipleship in small groups is that church is meant to be participatory. As we saw earlier in chapter 6, Paul taught that *each* member had an essential part in the edification of others according to his or her giftedness (1 Cor 12-14; Rom 12; Eph 4). He placed a high emphasis on participation because each person had a contribution to make. This level of participation is not easy in larger church gatherings but is more achievable in small groups.

The value of small groups in the life of the church is evidenced by the likes of Wesley, with his famous class meeting groups.[18] Luther's commitment to small group discipleship among believers is demonstrated in his use of home devotions, his practice of preaching in the home to his family and guests, his "Table Talk," and his authorization for the spiritual care of one Christian for another, through teaching, consolation, confession and absolution.[19]

Catechesis, which we mentioned in chapter 2, has also been an important discipleship tool. It began as a "whole of life" form of group discipleship for new believers but, in subsequent centuries, the term became more associated with the mastery of the propositional aspects of faith. It was used extensively in the post-apostolic church, during the Reformation in the sixteenth century and amongst the puritans in the seventeenth century.[20] According to Bryon Hollon, catechesis has traditionally had four elements: (1) the overarching narrative of Scripture, (2) the Apostles' Creed, (3) the Lord's Prayer (4) and the Ten Commandments.[21] John Wesley's groups broadened the focus of their ongoing form of discipleship to include the imitation of Christ, sharing the gospel and caring for the needy.[22]

One to one discipleship also has an unbroken history of effectiveness in supporting Christian growth and maturity. Most recently this has taken the name of "mentoring" which, Rick Lewis suggests, has arisen in response to the neglect of more holistic forms of discipleship:[23]

> Mentoring appeals to post-moderns because it goes beyond what a person knows to the condition of a person's soul. Mentoring gives people space and time, within the context of a sacred relationship, to journey toward transformation not by the power of propositional truth but by the power of the Spirit of truth. A Christian mentor is not so much a person with the right answers as a person with the right questions who walks the road of discovery with others.[24]

In one sense, Jesus' discipleship of those who followed him was an unrepeatable process. Yet, in the years following his ascension and across the centuries since, we have seen local churches intentionally take up aspects of his discipling ministry. No one of these dimensions of discipleship, and certainly no one person seeking to disciple others, can even begin to replicate what Jesus offered. Yet, there remains his promise that he is with us, and his assurance that he is still is the business of making disciples.

Reflection questions 7.2
1) What do you think is the most important insight regarding discipleship emerging from this survey of Scripture and tradition?

2) What does this survey of Scripture and tradition tell you about discipleship in your church?

Step 3: Wisdom

This brief survey of discipleship in Scripture and tradition has hopefully provided a good sense of the unchanging what and why of encouraging believers to grow in Christlikeness but the "how" of discipleship has proved to be far more flexible. Even Jesus' first disciples knew this all too well with their view of discipleship being revolutionised by Pentecost and the coming of the Holy Spirit. Then within a few short decades, they had transitioned from the largely oral transmission of the Apostles' teaching concerning Jesus' life and ministry to writing down "all that Jesus did and taught from the beginning until the day when he was taken up to heaven" (Acts 1:1-2). The arrival of the printing press in the fifteenth century, together with growing levels of literacy and the availability of discipleship materials in their own language, meant believers could read discipleship materials in the comfort of their own home in their own time. Discipleship became more individualised and disconnected from the social context of the church with both positive and negative consequences. Believers have had increasing access to information related to being disciples of Jesus, but many have lost the relationships and accountability that come from discipleship in community.

The Digital Revolution

As we began to discuss in chapter 5 on Vibrant Faith, the digital revolution has also potentially transformed discipleship.[25] Just as the printing press radically transformed discipleship, the Internet and digitisation of content has had a major impact on not just how we live, but how people are discipled. Many now access the Scriptures, and the wealth of online resources including Bible studies and blogs, through their smart phones freely and on demand. Of particular importance has been increased access to video materials through platforms like YouTube. Whereas previously discipleship was largely conducted within a church context, or at least a geographical location, disciples now have access to blogs and video input from people located in quite different contexts. Some local churches may now feel that they are in a struggle to disciple their own members before they are discipled by someone else through the Internet.

Those who consider "online church" and its associated discipleship an oxymoron or worse, raise issues such as the necessity of physical community as context,[26] a suspicion that online discipleship requires less commitment, and that consistency and accountability are lacking.[27] There are certainly theological challenges regarding the incarnational nature of salvation and the embodiedness of "normal" human relationality as it appears in Scripture, but many of those supporting the development of online forms of discipleship attempt to steer a course which sees online resourcing as a support and/or substitute when in-person worship and discipleship are not possible. Dave Adamson prefers the term "enhancement" and argues strongly that, given the online environment is now the "place" so many people inhabit, it is exactly where we should "go":

> I do not believe online church could or should replace attending a brick-and-mortar, physical church building. Ever. But, I do believe online technology can be—and should be—a tool to enhance the physical church... Leveraged properly, it can help introduce and connect the local community to your church, it can be used to partner with parents to help them to teach their kids and teenagers about faith, and it can be a key component of your church's discipleship strategy.[28]

Principles of adult learning indicate that approaches which are contextual and interactive are more likely to successfully engage "learners,"[29] and the kind of "transformative learning" that discipleship aims for will include reflection on life experience and critical thinking about the substance of faith in "communities of learning."[30] It would appear that the increasing potential for interactivity on social media and other platforms will better support such engagement beyond simply offering online versions of Sunday services.

One further development emerging from the digital revolution is the growth in podcasts. In 2020, 37% of Americans (age 12+) listened to at least one podcast each month, up from 32% in 2019. It is estimated that in 2020, 100 million people listened to a podcast each month and this is expected to reach 125 million in 2022.[31] There are now thousands of Christian podcasts that can potentially disciple believers. Because people can listen to a podcast while doing something else, like commuting or exercising, Christians can find time to listen to podcasts even if they are unlikely to find the time to access internet videos or blogs. Podcasts have enormous potential to transform discipleship, and it may be worth local churches considering the provision of recommendations for those seeking discipleship resources to encourage them to access those that are appropriate to their stage of growth and interests. Operating along the lines of traditional book clubs, opportunities to reflect on the content of podcasts in virtual or face to face small groups may, as we saw above, heighten the effectiveness of these discipleship tools. Such engagement may also help to avoid the loss of connection and influence which is vital to local church communities.

Revealing the Dimensions of Discipleship in the Local Church

One of the most significant insights into discipleship in recent decades was generated by the "Reveal" research conducted by the Willow Creek Association.[32] This research, based on data from 4943 surveys in 2007, and confirmed by tens of thousands of participants since, identified that practices such as daily prayer, Bible reading, serving, evangelism and love for God and others were strongly related to people's relationship with Christ.[33] As people moved from exploring Christianity, to growing in Christ, to being close to Christ, and then finally being Christ-centred, so their spiritual behaviours and attitudes became more Christlike.[34] The researchers concluded that spiritual growth is all about increasing relational closeness to Christ.[35] That is not surprising. What *was* surprising is that higher levels of participation in church activities did not seem to drive spiritual growth in more mature Christians. The role of their church in the spiritual growth of believers is summarised in the following table:

Stage of Spiritual Growth	Exploring Christianity	Growing in Christ	Close to Christ	Christ Centred
Role of Church in Spiritual Growth	Weekend services are critical. Interpersonal connection is important.	Weekend services remain important. Small groups rise in importance.	Weekend services decline in importance. Small groups drop in importance. Serving becomes more important.	The church provides the opportunity for service. Serving others becomes even more important.

This does not mean that churches have nothing to offer those who are further down the track in following Jesus. At each stage there are important things that local churches can do to keep their people on the move, progressing through the stages outlined above and preventing them from becoming "stalled" or "dissatisfied."[36] Moving from exploring Christ to growing in him, for example, requires "a clear set of next steps" which provide basic input on basic beliefs and practices such as baptism and communion, an introduction to personal spiritual practices, exploration of their spiritual gifts and serving opportunities, and training in basic evangelism.[37] At the other end of the spectrum, those who are Christ-centred, whilst mostly taking personal responsibility for their own continued growth, appreciate being challenged to continue to surrender their lives to Christ day by day and to serve others both within and beyond the church community.[38]

Whole Life Discipleship

Another factor to consider in your church's approach to discipleship is to ask the question, "What are we discipling people *for*?" As discussed in Chapter 3, the Whole Life Discipleship Movement has highlighted the importance of discipling people not just for their church life, but for their *whole* lives, especially on their "frontlines."[39] In other words, are we discipling people for life *inside* the church, or for their life *outside* the church? The London Institute of Contemporary Christianity,[40] Made to Flourish,[41] and the Theology of Work Project[42] are just three organisations which have done a great job producing resources to help churches disciple people not just for the hours when they are gathered at church services or church ministries but for the over 90% of their week when they are on their frontlines.

Short Term Missions

Another piece of wisdom emerging from social scientific research is the role of short-term mission trips in discipleship. Increased disposable income, inexpensive and efficient air travel, and improved communication have made short-term (from weeks up to a year) cross-cultural missions a distinct possibility for many Australians. It might also surprise you to know that the major beneficiaries of short-term mission trips are not those who are ministered to, but the short term missionaries themselves.[43] There has been much research into short-term missions, including some which demonstrates that cross-cultural missionaries report increased religious participation and solidified religious beliefs as a result of the trip.[44] Other research has indicated that people who go on short-term mission trips into cross-cultural contexts demonstrate significant positive changes in their beliefs, attitudes and behaviour as a result of the experience.[45] Those who have participated in "beach missions" and similar short-term missionary activities can testify to similar results.

So, short-term mission activities are great discipleship tools. The research suggests that pre- and post-trip discipleship activities are important to sustain the change beliefs, attitudes and behaviours.[46] Even if churches are unable to organise short-term mission trips themselves, they can play a crucial role in this preparation and follow-up. In addition to churches sending teams, there are many mission organizations that facilitate short-term missions.

Reflection Questions 7.3
1) What does this survey of human wisdom tell you about discipleship?

2) What does this survey of human wisdom tell you about discipleship in *your* church?

Step 4: Orthopraxy

Central to the idea of discipleship, or what Paul calls growing into maturity, is the idea of Christ-likeness. It is more than just knowing, it is being. Discipleship is not just something that happens in the intellect, but something reflected in attitudes and actions. Discipleship not only occurs through teaching but through relationship, experience, modelling and imitation. It is not limited to Sunday mornings but is manifest in the whole of life.

Hopefully this chapter has highlighted three things regarding discipleship. First, discipleship is the responsibility of the local church, and it is incredibly important. Hence the significance of being intentional. The advent of the Internet and the digitisation of content means that believers can be discipled by people they have never met. Although this may have some have advantages, it may also be problematic because it removes the interpersonal and communal dimensions of discipleship, and potentially leaves the local church out of the process. It is important to recognise, harness and address this trend in ways appropriate to your context.

Second, we should note there have always been a variety of tools for discipleship. Preaching, catechesis, small groups, mentoring, private reading, podcasts, and short-term mission trips are all possible avenues for discipleship in the local church. We encourage you not to assume that discipleship only occurs in certain ways or that it happens automatically.

Third, the Reveal research, and your own personal experience, should highlight that discipleship varies depending how far are you are along the journey. What works for a new believer may not work as well for the mature disciple. This underlines the importance of a thoughtful and flexible approach to fostering discipleship in your church.

Reflection Questions 7.4
1) What do you feel is the most important insight regarding discipleship generated by this chapter?

2) Is there anything you are unsure of or disagree with?

3) What do you feel is the most important insight on discipleship *for your church* generated by this chapter?

4) What else could you do to foster discipleship in your church?

Step 5: Action

As recorded in Matthew 28 Jesus considered that making disciples was of the utmost importance. And the local church has a crucial role to play in this mission. So it is important that local churches are thoughtful and intentional about how they foster discipleship. Here is a process which you might like to use or adapt for your context:

1) Gather together as a leadership and pray for the discernment of God's wisdom for your church with respect to its discipleship.

2) Share together your answers to Reflection Questions 7.4.

3) Individually, write down your answer to the following question: What should our church *do* to foster discipleship? You might come up with up to five suggestions. Try to make your suggestions as specific as possible. For example, rather than just saying "disciple young people," you could suggest something like "Establish a mentoring program across the church" or "Organise an annual short term mission trip."

4) Go around the group and have each member suggest one action the church could take to foster discipleship in your church. Write the suggestion on a whiteboard or similar media. If your suggestion has already been made put a tick next to it on the whiteboard and then share your next suggestion.

5) When everyone has shared all of their suggestions, each member in the group is allocated three votes. (You might like to allocate each member three self-adhesive dots for this activity.) Each member can then use their votes. They can allocate all three votes to the same suggestion or utilise them across a number of suggestions.

6) Tally up the dots and you will have an indication of what, as a leadership team, might be a good action step to take to develop discipleship in your church. Pray again and then decide which action steps you wish to take. Two or three is probably all that you can attempt at one time. Still, keep a record of your suggestions because you may be able to come back to them next year.

Conclusion

Our introduction to this chapter outlined the process for acquiring Australian citizenship. You'll remember that there are things to know, values and attitudes to learn and express, and actions to undertake. A solemn commitment to all this is expressed through a pledge of allegiance. Discipleship – growing into our citizenship of the kingdom of God – requires nothing less.

The gospel of the kingdom of God means that people are being called to submit to the rightful king ship of God. Jesus says:

> "Not everyone who calls out to me, 'Lord! Lord!' will enter the Kingdom of Heaven. Only those who actually do the will of my Father in heaven will enter." (Matt 7:21)

In other words, living in the kingdom means being a disciple of Christ – someone who increasingly does the will of God and becomes like Jesus. And the local church has a crucial role in this process.

Stephen Covey famously said, "the main thing is to keep the main thing the main thing."[47] And the main thing for the church is making disciples. But it is an intrinsically difficult activity. True discipleship is profoundly countercultural calling for self-sacrifice rather than self-gratification. And it is a lifelong pursuit. Yet, the local church, through the empowerment of the Holy Spirit, has been making disciples of Jesus for over 2000 years.

The church, however imperfectly, does continue to produce people who imitate and manifest the words, attitudes and actions of Jesus in their local context. It is a task of the utmost importance which continues to call the church to the utmost diligence in its pursuit.

Those aspiring to Australian citizenship have a booklet to follow. We have Jesus Christ. How much better is that?!

Chapter Endnotes

1. Dallas Willard, "The Gospel of the Kingdom and Spiritual Formation," in *The Kingdom Life: A Practical Theology of Discipleship and Spiritual Formation* (Colorado Springs: NavPress, 2010), Loc. 866.

2. *Australian Citizenship: Our Common Bond* (Commonwealth of Australia, 2020), https://immi.homeaffairs.gov.au/citizenship-subsite/files/our-common-bond-testable.pdf.

3. Ruth Powell et al., "Models of Church Vitality: A Literature Review," *NCLS Occasional Paper* 39 (2019): 13.

4. Gerhard Kittel, "Ἀκολουθέω, Ἐξ-, Ἐπ-, Παρ-, Συνακολουθέω," in *Theological Dictionary of the New Testament* (Grand Rapids: Eerdmans, 1964), 213.

5. Michael J. Wilkins, *Following the Master: A Biblical Theology of Discipleship* (Grand Rapids: Zondervan, 2010), 95.

6. Jeannine K. Brown, "Living Out Justice, Mercy, and Loyalty: Discipleship in Matthew's Gospel," in *Following Jesus Christ: The New Testament Message of Discipleship for Today*, ed. John Goodrich and Mark Strauss (Grand Rapids: Kregel Publications, 2019), 31.

7. M. Eugene Boring, "The Gospel of Matthew," in *New Interpreter's Bible*, ed. Leander E. Keck, vol. 8 (Nashville: Abingdon Press, 1994), 503.

8. Church practices from the NT on have differed regarding whether baptism is in the name of Father, Son and Spirit or in Jesus' name alone. See, for example, Acts 2:38; 8:16; Romans 6:3, 4; Galatians 3:27; Colossians 2:12.

9   George R. Beasley-Murray, *Baptism in the New Testament* (Grand Rapids: Eerdmans, 1962), 90.

10 Wilkins, *Following the Master*, 119.

11 Wilkins, 248.

12 Benjamin R. Wilson, "A Faith That Can Be Seen: Discipleship in Acts," in *Following Jesus Christ: The New Testament Message of Discipleship for Today*, ed. John Goodrich and Mark Strauss (Grand Rapids: Kregel Publications, 2019), 107.

13 Wilkins finds examples of such groups among the ongoing fellowship of the Apostles, the "pillars" of the church in Jerusalem, and the groups of those who travelled with Paul on his missionary journeys. See: Wilkins, *Following the Master*, 279.

14 After Jesus, Paul provides the preeminent NT example of this. Andreas J. Kostenberger, "Faithful Stewardship in God's Household: Discipleship in the Letters to Timothy and Titus," in *Following Jesus Christ: The New Testament Message of Discipleship for Today*, ed. John Goodrich and Mark Strauss (Grand Rapids: Kregel Publications, 2019), 223.

15 C.H. Spurgeon, "Characteristics of Christ's Disciples," The Spurgeon Center, 1882, https://www.spurgeon.org/resource-library/sermons/characteristics-of-christs-disciples/#flipbook/.

16 Ray E. Atwood, *Masters of Preaching: The Most Poignant And Powerful Homilists In Church History* (Lanham: Hamilton Books, 2012), 10.

17 Robert Banks, *Paul's Idea of Community: The Early House Churches in Their Cultural Setting* (Exeter: Paternoster, 1980), 60-61.

18 D Michael Henderson, *John Wesley's Class Meeting: A Model for Making Disciples* (Rafiki Books, 2016).

19 David John Zersen, "Lutheran Roots for Small Group Ministry," *Currents in Theology and Mission* 8, no. 4 (1981): 236.

20 J. I. Packer and Gary A. Parrett, *Grounded in the Gospel: Building Believers the Old-Fashioned Way* (Grand Rapids: Baker Books, 2010).

21 Bryan Hollon, "Catechesis and Christian Discipleship," *Knowing & Doing* Spring (2019), https://www.cslewisinstitute.org/Catechesis_and_Christian_Discipleship.

22 Bill Hull, *The Complete Book of Discipleship: On Being and Making Followers of Christ* (Colorado Springs: NavPress, 2006), 103-4.

23 Rick Lewis, *Mentoring Matters: Building Strong Christian Leaders, Avoiding Burnout, Reaching the Finishing Line* (Oxford: Monarch Books, 2009), 64.

24 Lewis, 66.

25 Bex Lewis, "The Digital Age: A Challenge for Christian Discipleship?" (paper presented at the Proceedings of the European Conference on Social Media (July, 10-11 2014, Brighton, UK), 2014).

26 Ronald L. Giese Jr, "Is 'Online Church' Really Church? The Church as God's Temple," *Themelios* 45, no. 2 (2020), https://www.thegospelcoalition.org/themelios/article/is-online-church-really-church-the-church-as-gods-temple/.

27 Collin Hansen, "Discipled by Everyone and No One: Is the Internet Good for the Church?," Desiring God, 2022, https://www.desiringgod.org/articles/discipled-by-everyone-and-no-one.

28 Dave Adamson, *MetaChurch: How to Use Digital Ministry to Reach People and Make Disciples* (Cumming: Orange, 2022), 36.

29 Annita Nugent, Jason M. Lodge, Annemaree Carroll, Rupert Bagraith and Pankaj Sah, *Higher Education Learning Framework: An Evidence Informed Model for University Learning* (Brisbane: The University of Queensland, 2019), 3.

30 Ros Stuart-Buttle, *Virtual Theology, Faith and Adult Education: An Interruptive Pedagogy* (Newcastle upon Tyne: Cambridge Scholars Publishing, 2013), 39, https://search.ebscohost.com/login.aspx?direct=true&db=nlebk&AN=632107&site=ehost-live&scope=site.

31 Brad Adgate, "As Podcasts Continue to Grow in Popularity, Ad Dollars Follow," Forbes, https://www.forbes.com/sites/bradadgate/2021/02/11/podcasting-has-become-a-big-business/?sh=74d0b3772cfb.

32 Greg L. Hawkins and Cally Parkinson, *Reveal: Where Are You?* (Barrington: Willow Creek Resources, 2007).

33 See more on these in Chapter 5.

34 Greg L. Hawkins and Cally Parkinson, *Move: What 1,000 Churches Reveal about Spiritual Growth* (Grand Rapids: Zondervan, 2017), 20.

35 Hawkins and Parkinson, 33-41.

36 Hawkins and Parkinson, 169–79.

37 Hawkins and Parkinson, 136.

38 Hawkins and Parkinson, 83–86.

39 Frontlines include workplaces, schools, clubs and non-Christian friends and relatives.

40 https://licc.org.uk/

41 https://www.madetoflourish.org/

42 https://www.theologyofwork.org/

43 Brian M. Howell, *Short-Term Mission: An Ethnography of Christian Travel Narrative and Experience* (Downers Grove: IVP Academic, 2012).

44 Jenny Trinitapoli and Stephen Vaisey, "The Transformative Role of Religious Experience: The Case of Short-Term Missions," *Social Forces* 88, no. 1 (2009).

45 Randy Friesen, "The Long-Term Impact of Short-Term Missions," *Evangelical Missions Quarterly* 41, no. 4 (2005).

46 Ibid.

47 Stephen R. Covey, A. Roger Merrill, and Rebecca R. Merrill, *First Things First* (New York: Simon and Schuster, 1995), 75.

Chapter 8
Caring for the Young

Introduction
In Matthew chapters 18 and 19, in quick succession, we read two accounts of Jesus' encounters with children:

> At that time the disciples came to Jesus and asked, "Who, then, is the greatest in the kingdom of heaven?" ² He called a little child to him and placed the child among them. ³ And he said: "Truly I tell you, unless you change and become like little children, you will never enter the kingdom of heaven. ⁴ Therefore, whoever takes the lowly position of this child is the greatest in the kingdom of heaven. ⁵ And whoever welcomes one such child in my name welcomes me. (Matt 18:1-5)

> ¹³ Then people brought little children to Jesus for him to place his hands on them and pray for them. But the disciples rebuked them. ¹⁴ Jesus said, "Let the little children come to me, and do not hinder them, for the kingdom of heaven belongs to such as these." ¹⁵ When he had placed his hands on them, he went on from there. (Matt 19:13-15)

Here, Jesus, in his own inimitable style, conveys two vital aspects of the kingdom at once. Firstly, we know that in this ancient context children were socially powerless and dependent.[1] Jesus uses this cultural "given" to proclaim that the posture for entry into God's kingdom needs to be like that of a child: humble, receptive and dependent. The lesson is one which often recedes as we grow in knowledge and experience of God's kingdom, but it's worth asking ourselves on a regular basis, "Am

I/Is our church maintaining a child-like trust in God? And is the gospel of the kingdom we preach one which encourages these child-like qualities?" When a student asked Karl Barth to summarise his life's work, he is reported to have replied with the words of a simple children's song: "Jesus loves me, this I know, for the Bible tells me so."[2] Such an approach (as Barth clearly demonstrated!) doesn't preclude the kind of theological thought or strategic action we've explored in this book, but it does say something important about the relational posture we adopt before God as we go about them. This is a vital part of learning to live kingdom shaped lives in our kingdom shaped churches.

But, secondly, the story also indicates that, unlike the disciples, Jesus greatly values children and his actions here are as much an enactment of the kingdom coming as his healing and teaching. The laying on of hands was normally associated with healing but here it suggests identification, acceptance and affection.[3] William Strange concludes, "What happens to a child, and to a child's faith is a matter of great consequence to those who are in the kingdom of God... In God's sight their worth cannot be exaggerated."[4] We should be both challenged and encouraged by Jesus' declaration that "Whoever welcomes one such child in my name welcomes me" (Matt 18:5).

But in addition to this kingdom-shaped imperative for the care of children, there are at least three other reasons why churches should focus on caring for their young people.

First, the children of church members represent the "ripe fruit" of the harvest. Many churches focus on reaching out to their non-Christian community in order to evangelise and grow. However, as good as this is, it sometimes means we underestimate the importance of discipling the children and youth already in their congregation. The NCLS has identified that retaining young adults is one of the key ways that churches grow.[5]

Second, if a young person makes a decision to become a follower of Jesus it is likely to shape their entire life. U.S. research by the Barna group indicates that nearly half of all Americans who accept Jesus Christ as their saviour do so before reaching the age of 13 (43%), and that two out of three born again Christians (64%) made that commitment to Christ before their 18th birthday.[6] Similarly, Australia's generation of young adults should be an important focus for the Church not just because of their demographic size, but also because of their openness to spiritual issues.[7]

Third, Australian churches need to care for young people because the future of many churches is at stake. The statistics on the drop out of youth and young people from church life is frightening. Almost all of attenders' children aged under 10 years attend church, but by the time they pass through secondary school and into young adulthood, around 40% may have ceased to attend.[8] This means that on the whole, the Australian church is ageing, and some denominations are ageing even more rapidly. Almost two in three in the Builders generation (63%) identify with Christianity, but only one in three Generation Y (32%) do so.[9] In 2016, 48% of Australian church attenders were aged 60 years and over, while only 13% were aged 15-29 years.[10]

Positive care for children, youth and young adults is vital to retaining young adults.[11] Hence, caring effectively for children, youth and young adults is crucial for the life of the kingdom and the survival of your church and the Church in Australia. But how can we do it better?

Step 1: Context

If you, as a church leadership, are concerned about the lack of children, youth and young adults in your church, you are not alone. Many churches recognise the sobering truth that organisations are only ever one generation away from extinction. Many churches have just a handful of children, youth and young adults. Others have none at all.

So, why are young people being lost to the church? David Kinnaman, based on his research amongst 18-29 year-olds in the U.S., identifies three groups of young people who have disconnected from the church:[12]

- Nomads: They walk away from church engagement but still consider themselves Christians.
- Prodigals: They lose their faith, describing themselves as "no longer Christian."
- Exiles: They are still invested in their Christian faith but feel stuck (or lost) between culture and the church. They say, "I want to find a way to follow Jesus that connects with the world I live in." They believe that God is more at work outside the church than inside, and they want to be part of that.

According to the research these young adults believe the Church is:[13]

- Overprotective — the church demonises everything outside of the church (especially movies, music and video games) and ignores the problems of the real world. This "risk-free" Christianity encourages young people to explore other more thrilling alternatives.
- Shallow — the church is boring because it is not relevant to me or prepare me for real life.
- Anti-science — the church is too confident that it knows all the answers and is out of step with the scientific world we live in. According to research cited in Kinnaman's book, although more than half of churchgoing 13 to 17-year-olds in America are looking at science related careers only one out of 100 youth workers talked about issues of science in the previous year.[14]
- Repressive — the church is concerned with rules not freedom. "We need to initiate respectful, frank (not vulgar or self-congratulatory) conversations that will help young people develop a deep, nuanced, and liveable sexual ethic…"[15]
- Exclusive — the church is not accepting of gays and lesbians and are afraid of the beliefs of other faiths. This means that many young people feel forced to choose between their faith and their friends.
- Doubtless — the church is not the place to ask my most pressing life questions. Nearly a quarter of American 18 to 29-year-olds have significant intellectual doubts about their faith but many don't feel they can raise those doubts in church.

Your NCLS church life Summary Profile includes a question about what aspects of the church are most valued. One of the options is "Ministry to Children or Youth." Where does this value rate in your church? Your NCLS Summary Profile will also give you some valuable information about caring for young people at your church including a graph showing the age distribution of your church compared to your community.

Reflection questions 8.1
1) What are your conclusions from your review of the NCLS data for your church?

2) Identify some nomads, prodigals and exiles who have been a part of your church community but who are no longer so. Do you know why?

3) Look through the terms identified by Kinnaman used by young adults to describe the Church. Do any of these apply to your church?

4) Look at the age make-up of your leadership group. Does it show you anything?

Step 2: Scripture and Tradition

Some might be surprised to know that the notion of adolescence is a fairly recent development. In the ancient world, and in many parts of the developing world today, there was no intermediate stage between childhood and adulthood. There was just one transition from being a child, when you were primarily supported by your parents, to being an adult when you left home, or moved to your own part of the home, and formed a new family and supported yourself. And so, from a sociological point of view there may be differences in the way we look at children's, youth and young adults' ministry, but from a biblical perspective there is not.

The crucial verses about the discipleship of young people in the Bible come from Deuteronomy 6:

> [4] Hear, O Israel: The Lord our God, the Lord is one. [5] Love the Lord your God with all your heart and with all your soul and with all your strength. [6] These commandments that I give you today are to be on your hearts. [7] Impress them on your children. Talk about them when you sit at home and when you walk along the road, when you lie down and when you get up. [8] Tie them as symbols on your hands and bind them on your foreheads. [9] Write them on the doorframes of your houses and on your gates.

The language of "teach them diligently" and "as you walk" reflect two dimensions of the discipleship of young people — deliberate and incidental. The word translated "impress" (6:7) was used to describe the work of a craftsman engraving an image. Parents are meant to "impress" God's commandments on their children's hearts. But discipleship is to also occur incidentally in the natural flow of life. It is not confined to certain periods of the day but is integrated into every part of family life. The word translated "you" in verses 7-9 is the second person singular. Although ancient Israel was clearly a collectivist culture, here the emphasis was on the responsibility of each parent to disciple their children. Although, as we shall see, the community of faith is also important, the primary responsibility rested with parents.

Another encouragement for incidental learning is in Joshua 4. God commands the people to carry stones across the river Jordan so that:

> [6]"In the future, when your children ask you, 'What do these stones mean?' [7] tell them that the flow of the Jordan was cut off before the ark of the covenant of the Lord. When it crossed the Jordan, the waters of the Jordan were cut off. These stones are to be a memorial to the people of Israel forever." (Josh 4:6-7)

Symbolic monuments like this, and the re-enactment of rituals like the Passover and the other feasts served to remind the community of their story of redemption. Religious symbols, including rituals and monuments, as well as reflecting obedience, were also to be used as stimulants for faith-based conversation. And note, it is "when" not "if" the children ask their parents about the meaning of the symbols and rituals. When young people share in the activities of their parents their inclination is usually (if not annoyingly!) to ask "why?" By intentionally building symbols of redemption (monuments or rituals) into everyday life, families foster fertile ground for faith conversations.

But the elders of the Israelite community also took responsibility for the discipleship of the next generation. As we read in Psalm 78:1-8, the psalmist takes on his responsibility to proclaim the history of redemption to the next generation:

> My people, hear my teaching;
> listen to the words of my mouth.
> ² I will open my mouth with a parable;
> I will utter hidden things, things from of old—
> ³ things we have heard and known,
> things our ancestors have told us.
> ⁴ We will not hide them from their descendants;
> we will tell the next generation
> the praiseworthy deeds of the Lord,
> his power, and the wonders he has done.
> ⁵ He decreed statutes for Jacob
> and established the law in Israel,
> which he commanded our ancestors
> to teach their children,
> ⁶ so the next generation would know them,
> even the children yet to be born,
> and they in turn would tell their children.
> ⁷ Then they would put their trust in God
> and would not forget his deeds
> but would keep his commands.

Thus it was the responsibility of the whole community to pass on the faith to the next generation not just the parents.

In the New Testament we see Jesus utilising both deliberate and incidental approaches of Deuteronomy 6 and adapting the rabbi-disciple model of learning for his purposes. The Gospels suggest that the disciples were young men, possibly teenagers.[16] Only Peter is identified as being married in a society where people married in their late teens. The traditional dating of the book of Revelation suggests that John was as young as 15 years old during the ministry of Jesus.

As we saw in Chapter 7, Jesus called these young men (Mark 3:14) and women (Luke 8:1-3[17], 10:39), "to be with him" and sent them out to preach and minister the kingdom. As important as his teachings were, Jesus sought to disciple through interpersonal relationship. It was as the disciples walked with Jesus, and witnessed his ministry, and asked questions, that they grew to maturity.

As we saw earlier, Jesus also demonstrated a counter-cultural attitude towards children. He invited children into his presence (Matt 18:2), rejecting the disciples' disdain for them. He used their play as an illustration (Luke 7:32) and healed them (Luke 8:54-55). Their value to Jesus was demonstrated by his declaration of the consequences for those who lead children astray:

> "If anyone causes one of these little ones—those who believe in me—to stumble, it would be better for them to have a large millstone hung around their neck and to be drowned in the depths of the sea." (Matt 18:6)

The New Testament also identifies the importance of the family in the discipleship of young people. Ephesians 6:4 urges fathers to not "exasperate your children; instead, bring them up in the training and instruction of the Lord." The verb translated "bring them up" relates to bodily nourishment and here implies the benefits of education. Children are to be treated with tenderness.[18] "Training" implies "to chasten" the child while "instruction" is correction by word of mouth. Both discipline and advice are encouraged in the home.

However, Colossians 3:20 ("Children, obey your parents in everything, for this pleases the Lord") suggests that children were present in the gathering of believers where the epistles were read. Coupled with the Titus 2 passage which encourages more mature members of the congregation to disciple the less mature members, we can see a multigenerational model of church life where the generations worship and build one another up together. This does not rule out the possibility of age specific worship and discipleship programs, but does validate the significance of multigenerational discipleship.

As we saw in the chapter on discipleship, an important tool through the history of the church has been catechesis. Although catechesis has sometimes been performed by local churches, during the Reformation parents were the chief catechists. In 1522, Luther preached a sermon entitled "Living as Husband and Wife," which became a pamphlet titled "The Estate of Marriage."[19] In it he said, "Most certainly father and mother are apostles, bishops, and priests to their children, for it is they who make them acquainted with the gospel."

However, church and parachurch organisations have emerged in recent centuries to complement the ministry of parents. The first Sunday School class was held in 1769 in England under the leadership of Hannah Ball, a disciple of John Wesley. A new age of ministry to the young people began with Christian Endeavour in 1881. Organisations like Youth for Christ which emerged in the 1940s were also very fruitful programs for young people in Australian churches. The unfortunate side effect of the emergence of these ministries has been that some parents have largely "outsourced" the discipleship of their children to the Church or parachurch organisations. Such outsourcing represents a distortion of the biblical model where the collective intergenerational church works with parents to disciple and care for the young people.

An overview of Scripture and church history would suggest that young people should be extraordinarily valued by the church and that their discipleship is both a deliberate and incidental activity stimulated by religious symbols and rituals. It should also be a cooperative process between the church (and sometimes the parachurch) and the family. At various times in history the pendulum of emphasis has swung one way or another. Whatever the situation in the 21st-century Australian context, it would appear the goal is for parents and church to partner in the discipleship of children, youth and young adults where they complement and support each other.

Reflection Questions 8.2

1) What do you think is the most important insight regarding caring for young people emerging from this survey of Scripture and tradition?

2) What does this survey of Scripture and tradition tell you about caring for young people *in your church*?

Step 3: Wisdom

The Passing on Faith Report[20] assimilates and presents the findings of 54 published studies on what makes a difference in the home when it comes to passing on faith. Unsurprisingly, the research largely affirms what the Bible says about caring for young people:

High quality relationships in the home are key to successful faith transmission: Adolescents and young adults who experience or who have experienced close, affirming, and accepting relationships with both parents are more likely to identify with the beliefs and practices of their parents.[21]

This is confirmed by Australian research which indicates almost half of all Australians who identify with spirituality or religion in some way (47%) are committed to the religion their parents or family brought them up in.[22] According to the NCLS, 58% of Australian church attenders aged 15 to 29 nominated their mother, and 46% nominated their father, as the person who showed them what faith was about.[23] Youth group leaders and friends are also influential with church attenders aged 15-29 likely to list their youth group leader (23%) and friends (24%) as the most important person to show them what faith is about.

Other Australian research indicates that conversations with others are by far the biggest prompt for young people thinking about spirituality and religion.[24] After conversations with people, social media is most influential for Generation Z (32%), whereas reading a book or article (25%) and personal unhappiness (22%) are most likely to prompt thinking about religion for Generation Y.

Smith, Ritz, and Rotolo,[25] identify certain faith practices that make a significant difference in nurturing the faith of young people at home:

- Reading the Bible as a family and encouraging young people to read the Bible regularly.
- Praying together as a family and encouraging young people to pray personally.
- Serving people in need as a family and supporting service activities by young people.
- Eating together as a family.
- Having family conversations about faith.
- Talking about faith, religious issues, and questions and doubts.
- Ritualizing important family moments and milestone experiences.
- Celebrating holidays and church year seasons at home.
- Providing moral instruction.

- Being involved in a faith community and participating regularly in Sunday worship as a family.

In addition, Kinnaman et al. identify five practices to help young people develop resilience as they live as exiles in a non-Christian culture:[26]

1) To form a resilient identity, experience intimacy with Jesus.

2) In a complex and anxious age, develop the muscles of cultural discernment.

3) When isolation and mistrust are the norms, forge meaningful, intergenerational relationships.

4) To ground and motivate an ambitious generation, train for vocational discipleship.

5) Curb entitlement and self-centred tendencies by engaging in countercultural mission.

Churches can partner with parents in the discipleship of their children by providing encouragement and resources to support these activities.

Churches should also reflect on how well they are providing young people with opportunities to minister in their church. The NCLS asked Australian churchgoers whether they were as involved as they would like to be at their local church.[27] The majority of each age group was happy with their current level of involvement (Builders 80%; Boomers 69%; Gen X 60%; Gen Y and Z 56%). However, some 31% of Generation Z (youth/ young adults), 32% of Generation Y (young adults) and 27% of Generation X (mid-life adults) said they would like to be more involved at their local church. Young adults have a tremendous amount to contribute to church life, but this research would suggest that one third of them are not getting the opportunity to do so.

Reflection Questions 8.3
1) What does this survey of human wisdom tell you about caring for young people?

2) What does this survey of human wisdom tell you about caring for young people in *your* church?

3) What resources and encouragement does your church provide for parents to help them disciple their children?

4) What ministries are the young people in your church exercising?

Step 4: Orthopraxy

The Fuller youth Institute has conducted extensive research and developed resources to help churches "grow young."[28] They identified 363 diverse congregations who had effective ministry to young people and identified six core commitments that these congregation shared.[29] They serve as a good summary of orthopraxy for churches looking to care for the young.

1) Unlock keychain leadership
   This means of sharing power with the right people at the right time. Instead of holding onto your authority, empower young people. Because you are so committed to your church you may hesitate to entrust it to other people, especially young people, in case they make mistakes. However, if we do not entrust our church to the younger generations, there may be no church left to entrust.

2) Empathize with today's young people
   Instead of judging or criticising young people, step into their shoes. Arrange to share a cup of coffee with a young person and ask them, "What is life like for you?" Try to understand, and so better love them.

3) Take Jesus' message seriously
   Instead of teaching a thin and moralistic message which poorly equips young Christians to resist the pressures of secularism, churches should teach a robust gospel focused message built on the redemptive narrative of the Bible. Further, Australian

research shows that even if young people don't love the church, they love Jesus.³⁰ Make Jesus the focus rather than the institutional church.

4) Fuel a "warm" community
As we have seen, personal relationships with parents and intergenerational communities are key for discipleship. Instead of just focusing on "cool" or superficial worship or programs, churches should seek to foster "warm" peer and intergenerational friendships.

5) Prioritize young people (and families) everywhere
Look for creative ways to tangibly support, resource and involve young people in all facets of your church. And remember, you cannot fool young people into believing you have made them a priority — it needs to be an authentic commitment to caring for the young as a priority.

6) Be the best neighbours
Instead of just condemning the world outside the church, equip young people to minister well in their schools, universities, clubs and workplaces. Young people are very concerned about social justice and the environment, and they want their church to be as well.

To this we would add two suggestions emerging from the theological discussion above:

1) Churches and parents should actively partner with one another in the discipleship of young people in their church.

2) Churches and parents should actively utilise "religious" symbols as a stimulus for significant faith discussions in day-to-day life.

Reflection Questions 8.4
1) What do you feel is the most important insight caring for young people generated by this chapter?

2) Is there anything in this chapter you are unsure of or disagree with?

3) What do you feel is the most important insight on caring for young people *for your church* generated by this chapter?

4) What else could you do to better care for young people in your church?

Step 5: Action

Here is a process which you might like to use or adapt to develop some action step towards better caring for young people in your church:

1) Gather together pray for the discernment of God's wisdom for your church with respect to caring for young people.

2) Share together your answers to Reflection Questions 8.4.

3) Individually, write down your answer to the following question: What should we do to better care for young people in our church? You might come up with up to five suggestions. Try to make your suggestions as specific as possible. For example, rather than just saying, "Be more supportive of parents," you could suggest something like "Running a parenting course specifically aimed at helping parents disciple their children" or "Introduce a children's story into our worship service to show children how much we value them."

4) Go around the group and have each member suggest one action the church could take to better care for young people. Write the suggestion on a whiteboard or similar media. If your suggestion has already been made put a tick next to it on the whiteboard and then share your next suggestion.

5) When everyone has shared all of their suggestions, each member in the group is allocated three votes. (You might like to allocate each member three self-adhesive dots for this activity.) Each member can then use their votes. They can allocate all three votes to the same suggestion or utilise them across a number of suggestions.

6) Tally up the dots and you will have an indication of what, as a leadership team, might be a good action step to take to better care for young people. Pray again and then decide which action steps you wish to take. Two or three is probably all that you can attempt at one time. Keep a record of your suggestions because you may be able to come back to them next year.

Conclusion

For those churches who have already lost their young people, the journey back to a multigenerational existence may be a challenging one. However, it is possible. Ian was involved in a church that took faith-based steps to attract and hold young people once again. Even though there was only a very small number of children in the congregation, the vestry at the back of the church building was converted into a "parent's room," a children's talk and Sunday school were scheduled each Sunday even if on some Sundays no children came to church. Gradually, as families joined the church, the children began to collect the offering and bring the Bible reading. Even though the church was small, it employed a children's worker to ensure there was quality children's ministry each Sunday. Over time, through persistence in prayer, and faith-based decision-making, the number of children in the church grew significantly.

So, there is hope for smaller churches which are unable to support a youth worker or even a youth group. Many churches throughout history, and in many parts of the world today, have neither. When this is the case, churches may partner with families in the discipling of their children through providing prayer, encouragement, intergenerational relationships and resources. As was exemplified during Covid lockdowns, such care might look very different from either traditional forms of child/youth focused ministry or those normally offered by larger churches but it can, nonetheless, be meaningful and fruitful. Churches of all sizes and types can effectively care for young people.

Whatever our context, everyone benefits! Children and young people are nurtured for faith and life. Parents and grandparents are encouraged and delighted to witness God at work in their children and grandchildren. The church is reminded that "the kingdom belongs to such as these" and learns to live its kingdom shaped life. And all together we play our part in Jesus' promise to build his church and God's commitment to establish the kingdom in every generation.

Chapter Endnotes

1. Craig S. Keener, *The Ivp Bible Background Commentary: New Testament*, Electronic ed. (Downers Grove: InterVarsity Press, 1993), Matt 19:13–15.

2. Roger Olsen has investigated the veracity of this comment and argues that Barth probably used it more than once on his trip to the USA in 1962. Roger E Olson, "Did Karl Barth Really Say 'Jesus Loves Me, This I Know…?,'" *My Evangelical Arminian Theological Musings* (blog), 2013, https://www.patheos.com/blogs/rogereolson/2013/01/did-karl-barth-really-say-jesus-loves-me-this-i-know/#disqus_thread.

3. R. T. France, *Matthew: An Introduction and Commentary*, Tyndale New Testament Commentaries (Nottingham: InterVarsity Press, 1985).

4. William A. Strange, *Children in the Early Church: Children in the Ancient World, the New Testament and the Early Church* (Eugene: Wipf and Stock, 2004), 57-58.

5. Peter Kaldor, John Bellamy, and Sandra Moore, *Mission under the Microscope: Keys to Effective and Sustainable Mission* (Adelaide: Openbook, 1995), 113-26.

6. The Barna Group, "Evangelism Is Most Effective among Kids," https://www.barna.com/research/evangelism-is-most-effective-among-kids/.

7. Mark McCrindle, *Emerging Trends, Enduring Truth: The Spiritual Attitudes of the New Generations* (Sydney: McCrindle Research, 2009).

8. Peter Kaldor, Keith Castle, and Robert Dixon, *Connections for Life: Core Qualities to Foster in Your Church* (Adelaide: Openbook, 2002), 47.

9   Mark McCrindle, *Faith and Belief in Australia* (Sydney: McCrindle Research, 2017).

10 Ruth Powell, Miriam Pepper, and Kathy Jacka Kerr, "An Ageing Church but Not Everywhere," National Church Life Survey, https://www.ncls.org.au/news/ageing-church.

11 Kaldor, Castle, and Dixon, 47.

12 David Kinnaman and Aly Hawkins, *You Lost Me: Why Young Christians Are Leaving Church ... And Rethinking Faith* (Grand Rapids: Baker, 2011).

13 Ibid., 92-93.

14 Ibid., 140.

15 Ibid., 162.

16 Otis Cary and Frank Cary, "How Old Were Christ's Disciples?," *The Biblical World* 50, no. 1 (1917).

17 "The rabbis refused to teach women and generally assigned them a very inferior place. But Jesus freely admitted them into fellowship, as on this occasion, and accepted their service." Leon Morris, *Luke: An Introduction and Commentary* (Grand Rapids: Eerdmans Publishing, 1988), 169.

18 A. Skevington Wood, "Ephesians," in *The Expositor's Bible Commentary: Ephesians through Philemon, Vol.11*, ed. Frank E. Gaebelein (Grand Rapids: Zondervan Publishing House, 1981), 82.

19 Martin Luther, *Martin Luther's Basic Theological Writings*, trans. William R. Russell, 3rd ed. ed. (Minneapolis: Fortress Press, 2012), Chapter 34.

20 Olwyn Mark, *Passing on Faith* (London: Theos, 2016).

21 Ibid., 12.

22 McCrindle, *Faith and Belief in Australia*, 15.

23 Kathy Jacka, Miriam Pepper, Nicole Ward, Ruth Powell and Sam Sterland, "Parents Remain the Most Valuable Role Models of Faith," http://ncls.org.au/news/parents-role-models-for-faith.

24 McCrindle, *Faith and Belief in Australia*, 19.

25 Christian Smith, Bridget Ritz, and Michael Rotolo, *Religious Parenting: Transmitting Faith and Values in Contemporary America* (Princeton University Press, 2019), 179.

26 David Kinnaman, Mark Matlock, and Aly Hawkins, *Faith for Exiles: 5 Ways for a New Generation to Follow Jesus in Digital Babylon* (Grand Rapids: Baker, 2019), 30, 34-35.

27 Kathy Jacka, Miriam Pepper, Ruth Powell and Sam Sterland, "Generations X, Y and Z Want to Be More Involved at Church," http://www.ncls.org.au/news/generations-xyz-more-involved-at-church.

28 Kara Eckmann Powell, Jake Mulder, and Brad Griffin, *Growing Young: Six Essential Strategies to Help Young People Discover and Love Your Church* (Grand Rapids: Baker Books, 2016); Fuller Youth Institute, *Growing Young Church Discussion Guide* (Pasadena: Fuller Youth Institute, 2016).

29 Powell, Mulder, and Griffin, 43.

30 McCrindle, *Faith and Belief in Australia*.

Chapter 9
Generous Giving

Introduction

Generous giving is not ultimately about resourcing Christian ministry. As a wise old Christian once said, "The Lord owns the cattle on a thousand hills (Psalm 50:9-10), and if he needed money, he could sell one." Churches need to be concerned about fostering generous giving because it is a reflection of the generosity that characterises the kingdom of God. The kingdom reflects the character of the King. God generously sustains and satisfies all creation. As the psalmist says in Psalm 104:

> [27] All creatures look to you
>   to give them their food at the proper time.
> [28] When you give it to them,
>   they gather it up;
> when you open your hand,
>   they are satisfied with good things.

Jesus reflected the generous character of his Father in Mark 6, where he feeds the five thousand:

> [42] They all ate and were satisfied, [43] and the disciples picked up twelve basketfuls of broken pieces of bread and fish.

There wasn't just sufficient to stop people from being hungry. They all ate and they were all satisfied by Jesus' abundant provision. Indeed there were large basketfuls of bread and fish left over. When discussing the tendency of humans to worry about economic needs, Jesus says:

> Therefore, I tell you do not worry about your life, what you will eat or drink; or about your body, what you will wear... But seek first his kingdom and his righteousness, and all these things will be given to you as well. (Matt 6:25, 33)

Focus on the kingdom, and all these other things will sort themselves out because God's kingdom is a kingdom of abundance.

Given that it reflects one of the key characteristics of the kingdom of God, generous giving is also a matter of discipleship — of growing into our kingdom citizenship. Christians who give generously of their time and money do so because they are filled with gratitude to God, because they want to be aligned with God's kingdom, because they trust in God to meet their needs even if they give away a lot of their resources, and for a range of other reasons.

But for many Christians, their finances are the last part of their lives to come under the reign of Christ. It is only as they learn to give generously that they see spiritual growth in these areas. And so churches need to be encouraging generous giving as a key part of their discipleship strategy even if those churches do not directly benefit.

So, even though God owns the cattle on a thousand hills, generous giving by disciples is the way that God primarily chooses to resource the ministry of local churches. Although disciples should be generous with their time and money in a whole range of worthwhile places as an expression of their Christian faith, this chapter will be looking specifically at how local churches can foster generous giving towards the ministry of their church.

Such consideration is timely for many Australian churches whose finances are a major source of concern. Research by the NCLS has shown that although in 2016, 53% of Australian churches reported having a stable financial base, 24% had a declining financial base, and another 8% were declining so seriously as to threaten their viability.[1] Churches with stable or declining financial bases need to be thinking seriously about generous giving within their congregations. For those who do have a more secure financial footing, a kingdom mindset will always be on the lookout for more funding to support new projects, the expansion of existing ministries, or the construction and maintenance of the buildings which house them.

Different denominations have quite different approaches to church giving. If you are part of a Pentecostal denomination, you are probably very comfortable with talking about money, even in church services. Other churches will be far more hesitant about the discussion of money, even at a leadership level. However, the distinctively generous nature of the kingdom of God, the relationship between wealth and discipleship and the importance of generous giving for church effectiveness and viability means that we need to think and talk about it seriously.

Step 1: Context

As with many of the dimensions of kingdom aligned church vitality we have looked at in this book, your last National Church Life Survey, if you participated in it, provides you with an excellent resource to inform your discussion of giving in your church. In your Church Profile in the section on "Sense of Belonging" there are some questions about financial giving. You should be able to identify the percentage of the congregation who say they are giving 10% or more of their net income in comparison to your previous NCLS survey and your denomination. There are also some questions relating to generosity in the "Service" Core Quality section of your Church Life Profile. Please carefully consider what you discover.

However, even if you do not have access to your NCLS survey, you should still have a wealth of data to inform your discussion. Simply graphing your average monthly giving over the last five years will likely reveal some interesting trends. Another useful exercise is to calculate your average giving per "giving unit." A giving unit is an individual, couple, or family who are a potential giver to your church. If you divide your total annual offering by the total number of giving units in your church, you will have your "average giving per giving unit." This is a helpful metric to consider and compare with past and future years.

It might also be helpful to consider the future financial needs or goals of your church. Are there any pressing and costly building maintenance issues on the horizon? What resources do you need to make steps towards fulfilling the kingdom aligned vision you developed earlier?

Reflection questions 9.1
1) What does our NCLS church life profile tell us about the giving in our church?

2) How comfortable are we, as a church, talking about money?

3) How comfortable are we, as a leadership, talking about money?

4) Does our church have any pressing needs or goals which need resourcing?

5) On a scale of 1 to 5, with 1 being catastrophic, and 5 being fantastic, how would you rate the finances of your church?

Step 2: Scripture and Tradition

As discussed earlier, the generous character of God finds expression in his kingdom on earth. But according to the New Testament this wonderfully abstract idea manifests itself in the very pragmatic giving of money to support ministry. It appears that Jesus' first disciples gave up their income in order to become his disciples. We have the record of Peter and his brother leaving their fishing trade in order to follow Jesus. Levi left his tax franchise. How did Jesus and the apostles support themselves? Luke 8:2-3 reports that Jesus' disciples were supported by Mary Magdalene, Joanna, the wife of Herod's steward, and Susanna. Jesus and his disciples had given up their paid work in order to minister. Luke seems to want to make the point that it was largely through the generous giving of these women that they were able to do so. Further, in Acts 16, Lydia offered support to Paul while he stayed in Philippi. In Romans 16:1-2, Phoebe is identified as a "benefactor" of many, including Paul. Kingdom inspired generosity can take many forms, but one important aspect of this is the giving of money to support people in Christian ministry.

In many Australian churches the discussion about giving generously is usually dominated by the practice of "tithe." Many think all believers should "tithe" 10% of their income to their local church and make special "offerings" in addition to that. Others are equally convinced tithing is not required for Christians.

The 20th-century emphasis on tithing can be traced to Chicago businessman Thomas Kane, who distributed pamphlets promoting tithing during the last quarter of the 19th century.[2] A 2017 Lifeway survey amongst American Protestants found that 83% of churchgoing adults and 72% of pastors said they believed tithing was a biblical command that still applied today.[3] However, nearly half of the churchgoers in the survey reported that they gave less than 10% to their church.

The practice of tithing is largely based on Old Testament examples. Abraham gave a tenth of his spoils of war to Melchizedek (Gen. 14:20). In Genesis 28:22, God met Jacob at Bethel and promised him covenant blessings and in response the patriarch promised God a tenth of everything God gave him. In ancient Israel, one tenth of the seed, fruit, and flocks were tithed to the Lord (Lev. 27:30-32; Deut. 14:22-24; cf. 2 Chron. 31:5-6; Neh. 13:5, 12). Those who didn't tithe were threatened with a curse, while those who did tithe were promised blessing (Mal. 3:8-10). Some scholars think the Israelites actually gave multiple tithes each year and that the amount given to the Lord exceeded 20%.[4] Regardless of these speculations, on the basis of this Old Testament practice, many Christians have been encouraged to "tithe" 10% of their income to their local church as the Israelites were required to tithe to the temple and the priests.

However, many believe that the tithe is not relevant to New Testament Christians for the following reasons:[5]

1) Believers are no longer under the Mosaic covenant (Rom. 6:14-15; 7:5-6; Gal. 3:15-4:7; 2 Cor. 3:4-18). The moral norms of the Old Testament are still in force today, but tithing is not among these commands.

2) The examples of Abraham and Jacob are descriptive, not normative patterns.

3) Tithes were given to the Levites and priests, but there are no Levites and priests in the new covenant.

4) The tithe is tied to the land Israel received under the old covenant.

5) If tithing is required today, how much should we give? The proportion given was probably more than 10% and closer to 20%.

6) When Jesus affirmed the tithe (Matt. 23:23; Luke 11:42), it was before the dawn of the new covenant.

7) Nowhere is tithing mentioned when commands to give generously are found in the New Testament.

Whether you believe the Old Testament principle of tithing applies to the contemporary church or not, there are some passages which unambiguously give guidelines for how Christians should give to their local church.[6]

Verses	Principles
1 Corinthians 9:14 [14] In the same way, the Lord has commanded that those who preach the gospel should receive their living from the gospel.	• Give to support the needs of those set aside for ministry.
1 Corinthians 16:1-2: Now about the collection for the Lord's people: Do what I told the Galatian churches to do. [2] On the first day of every week, each one of you should set aside a sum of money in keeping with your income, saving it up, so that when I come no collections will have to be made.	• Set aside a portion of your income each week whether that be for a special cause or weekly giving. • Give "in keeping with your income."
2 Corinthians 8:2-4 [2] In the midst of a very severe trial, their overflowing joy and their extreme poverty welled up in rich generosity. [3] For I testify that they gave as much as they were able, and even beyond their ability. Entirely on their own, [4] they urgently pleaded with us for the privilege of sharing in this service to the Lord's people.	• Give generously as much as you are able. • Give to share in the privilege of service to the Lord's people.

2 Corinthians 9:6-8 ⁶ Remember this: Whoever sows sparingly will also reap sparingly, and whoever sows generously will also reap generously. ⁷ Each of you should give what you have decided in your heart to give, not reluctantly or under compulsion, for God loves a cheerful giver. ⁸ And God is able to bless you abundantly, so that in all things at all times, having all that you need, you will abound in every good work.	• Give so that God can bless you abundantly (so that you can "abound in every good work.") • Decide in your heart what you will give. • Give cheerfully, not reluctantly or under compulsion.
Philippians 4:18 ¹⁸ I have received full payment and have more than enough. I am amply supplied, now that I have received from Epaphroditus the gifts you sent. They are a fragrant offering, an acceptable sacrifice, pleasing to God.	• Generous gifts are beautiful, sacred and pleasing to God.

One of Jesus' many teachings regarding money involves how you give it away:

> Be careful not to practice your righteousness in front of others to be seen by them. If you do, you will have no reward from your Father in heaven. ² So when you give to the needy, do not announce it with trumpets, as the hypocrites do in the synagogues and on the streets, to be honoured by others. Truly I tell you, they have received their reward in full. ³ But when you give to the needy, do not let your left hand know what your right hand is doing, ⁴ so that your giving may be in secret. Then your Father, who sees what is done in secret, will reward you (Matt 6:1-4).

In contrast to the public generosity of the Pharisees, Jesus tells his disciples to make their giving in private. Some churches interpret this verse as meaning that we should not recognise the contributions that donors make. But Jesus' words were directed at the *givers*, not the *receivers*. Certainly, generous givers should not call unnecessary attention to themselves. But

Jesus never taught his disciples to be ungrateful. In fact he expressed disappointment about the nine lepers whom he healed that did not return to give him thanks (Luke 17:11-19). In contrast, disciples should be overflowing with thankfulness (Col 2:7). This means that generous giving should be done privately *and* that churches should respond gratefully. We will come back to this later.

Church history is inconclusive in reaching conclusions about giving. Disciples in the earliest churches shared *all* their possessions (Acts 2:44-45). Irenaeus wrote in the second century,

> And for this reason they (the Jews) had indeed the tithes of the goods consecrated to him but those who have received liberty set aside all their possessions for the Lord's purposes, bestowing joyfully and freely not the less valuable portions of their property.[7]

However, Augustine (354-430) and subsequent church councils taught that Christians were to tithe.[8] Calvin was in favour of tithing, but Luther was against it. John Wesley (1703-1791) laid down a three-part rule for his Methodist followers in: "Gain all you can. Save all you can. Give all you can."[9] So, whether we embrace the concept of the tithe or not, generous giving is a theme throughout Scripture and church history.

Reflection questions 9.2
1) What do you think is the most important insight regarding giving emerging from this survey of Scripture and tradition?

2) What does this survey of Scripture and tradition tell you about *your* giving in your church?

Step 3: Wisdom

Research by the NCLS suggests that there is a disconnect between the expectation of church attenders and church leaders when it comes to giving. "Whilst most church leaders (63%) thought that tithing was a realistic expectation of church attenders, only about a third of attenders were of the same opinion."[10] This is an important insight into why many churches struggle to meet their budgets.

The NCLS research also identified that the biggest influencers on attender decisions about giving to their local church were, "A sense of gratitude for God's love and goodness" (39%) and "wanting to contribute to God's work in the world" (30%). "A sense of religious duty" (22%), obligation to support the church's work (15%), Bible teaching on giving (14%) and hearing about specific needs (13%) were also influential. However, there were significant differences in the main factors which influenced attenders to give to their local church between the denominations.[11]

Understanding Why People Give

Social science has a keen interest in philanthropy and the question of why people give away their money to causes. Based on their survey of the research into nurturing donors, Guy and Patton identify a number of things that donor nurturers can do to encourage giving.[12] We can carefully take these principles and adapt them to encourage generous giving in our churches in light of the deeper motivations that should move Christians:

1) Provide Need Satisfaction

    For many donors the satisfaction comes from helping the needy not the help given to the intermediary. Donors give in response to the need, not for the organisation that meets the need. By implication, people do not give to "the church" *per se*, they give to the *ministry* that the church performs out of their desire to help others. This is a subtle but important difference.

2) Generate Awareness That Needs Exist

    Donor nurturers should seek to generate awareness that the need exists and that it is "urgent and severe." People sometimes do not give generously to their local church because they are unaware that the need exists or that they need to act in response. In our information saturated world, a subtle message regarding a financial need in the church can easily get lost. Churches need to communicate clearly that a financial need exists.

3) Instil a Sense of Personal Responsibility

    Appeals to groups about financial needs are generally ineffective because of the "phenomenon of the diffusion of responsibility."[13]

Potential donors tend to think that someone else will meet the financial need unless they become aware of their personal responsibility. Instilling this personal responsibility is best done through face-to-face personal contact. Maturing disciples who are motivated by gratitude to God and the desire to join God's work, will give generously to causes that they recognise are their responsibility. Churches need to make the simple point that, "People in other churches will not make a financial contribution to your church."

4) Demonstrate Ability and Competence to Help
The donor wants to be sure that their donation will actually make a difference. In the same way, generous Christians want to make sure that when they give to a local church, the church will be able to use the money for effective ministry. They need to be convinced that the ministry they have been called to support will make a difference. Even wealthy Christians do not want to see their resources wasted.

5) Remove the Barriers
Even if a donor is motivated to give, the barriers to giving may be too much to overcome. Hence donor nurturers should make sure the giving is as easy as possible. In the same way, churches need to work hard to make sure that generous giving is as easy as possible.

Fostering Giving to Church

In encouraging generous church giving, Hoge et al. argue that the most common problems are inadequate communication of the financial needs of the congregation to the members and a low level of trust by many members in the policy-making processes of the congregation.[14] Often, portions of the congregation feel they are not being heard or are not being given all the information. Such feelings will deter generous giving. Having lay leaders manage the finances and lead the stewardship programs will help reduce any suspicions that the clergy are promoting giving solely out of self-interest (2 Cor 8:20: "We want to avoid any criticism of the way we administer this liberal gift.") Broad lay participation in the congregation's budgeting and priority setting will also contribute to a sense of ownership and responsibility. Full financial accountability and reporting will allay suspicions that the clergy or a few lay leaders are doing anything in secret.

Australian Anglican minister, Rod Irvine, recommends that churches develop a pledge system.[15] At an annual "Commitment Day," members of the church are invited to indicate the amount of money they would give to the church in the next year. This approach proved very successful at raising the generosity of giving at Irvine's church. He also advocated inviting people to commit themselves to "special offerings" for specific ministry projects in addition to their weekly giving to the church. Sometimes we assume that people will only give a fixed amount to God's work, and if we present them with multiple options, they will simply give the same total amount to a greater number of causes. However, this is not the case. "Generally, extra projects unlock more generosity."[16] For example, some people might be moved to give money for a new drum kit, while others will be more inclined to give to employ a children's worker and others will be moved to give to feed a child overseas. The more compelling causes grateful and kingdom-aligned disciples have, the more they will give.

Irvine also notes the importance of example. Church leaders need to lead the way in generous giving especially when it comes to big projects.[17] The amounts pledged by individual leaders need not be publicly identified, but the pledged contribution of the whole leadership team can be a huge encouragement for the rest of the congregation.

Reflection Questions 9.3
1) What does this survey of human wisdom tell you about fostering generous church giving?

2) What does this survey of human wisdom tell you about fostering generous church giving in *your* church?

Step 4: Orthopraxy
One of the important features of Practical Theology is that it is done at a local, contextual level. Just as individuals in the body of Christ are diverse, so the millions of local manifestations of Christ's body are also diverse. Although we share some essential things in common, there are many points where we will differ. Perhaps this is no more apparent that when it comes to the question of generous giving. Some churches already

do a tremendous job at encouraging generous giving. However, other churches are much more hesitant when it comes to talking about money and so fostering generous giving is a more challenging task. Whatever your context, here are a few suggestions on cultivating generosity in your church.[18]

Teach About It

The Bible talks a lot about money and generous giving. As a result, we should be talking and teaching a lot about money in local churches. Ian remembers when he was a new pastor in an older church and the preaching schedule called for him to preach on giving. He was very nervous, especially when after the service one of the outspoken members of the church walked purposefully towards him. She said, "Thank you for that sermon." A little taken aback Ian replied, "Thank you, I was a bit nervous about the topic." Enthusiastically she said, "No, that was great. In the old days preachers used to talk about money all the time. We need to hear more sermons like that." If we are committed to preaching and teaching the whole Bible, we will be committed to teaching and preaching about giving generously to reflect God's kingdom character and to serve his kingdom purposes.

Focus on Vision and Celebrate Changed Lives

Many of the people in your church want to make a difference in the lives of others. So keep the kingdom-aligned vision of the church in front of attenders and remind them that through their generous giving they are resourcing ministries that are changing lives, rather than just meeting a budget. Make sure to share stories of the way that the ministries of the church are changing lives. Remind church attenders that they are part of a team which is making an eternal difference.

Remember that Giving is Emotional

Giving to a ministry is an emotional activity because people are either going to feel excited and joyful or resentful and guilty about their giving. Your job is to make it a positive emotion. Let givers know that they can take great satisfaction in being able to express their gratitude to God and joining with God's kingdom work in the world.

Appreciate your givers

Most of us do not enjoy giving gifts that are not appreciated. Many churches never specifically thank their people for their financial contributions. Most generous givers do not want a public accolade for their giving. But simple expressions of gratitude can be greatly encouraging. It may be as simple as having someone write a letter to those who are giving generously to the church. For others a face-to-face meeting, with some hospitality, to share the difference their generosity is making in the lives of other people will be appropriate.

Be Financially Accountable

The finances of your church should be available for the whole congregation to see. Make it a point to make financial reports at regular intervals, to show that the church leaders are being transparent and accountable for how God's money is spent. You never want your people to question if their gifts are being used wisely. Clearly present the facts concerning your church's financial condition whether they are good or bad.

Teach Financial Stewardship

Many people in your church would like to give more, but they feel that they can't. Increased expectations, excessive debt, underemployment and a whole range of other factors might mean that people are in financial difficulties. However, if churches can disciple people in the realm of their finances, primarily through debt management/resistance and budgeting, people will have a stronger financial position and be better able to give generously to their local church.

Online Giving

In addition to these ideas, another issue for church leaderships to think about is the use of direct debit. One of the consequences of the Covid 19 lockdowns in 2020 and 2021 has been the growth of electronic giving in churches. Although it had already been a growing phenomenon, most churches stopped "passing the plate" during services and the levels of online giving sharply increased. Anecdotally, the level of online giving has remained higher for most churches. It requires an intentional act to cancel an automatic direct debit. Many Christians have decided to continue using online giving rather than going back to the old "manual" method.

Some have argued that although driven by practical circumstances, online giving is more aligned to the biblical concept of giving the "first fruits" (Prov. 3:9) of our income to the Lord. Others would argue that by setting up an automatic direct debit we are losing the sacred rhythm of giving. Perhaps maintaining an offering prayer or ritual as part of the worship service will address this to some degree.

However, even if we have theological reservations, online giving will remain a feature of church life. And one unintended consequence of online giving is that churches are able to identify who their regular donors are. Bank statements will usually indicate who has made deposits into the church's accounts. This is potentially beneficial in two ways. First, it enables the church leadership to identify who is *actually* committed to their church. Church commitment has often been measured by their attendance at public worship and perhaps formal church membership. However, given the increasing irregularity of church attendance, financial commitment to a local church is a perhaps more tangible and accurate measure. A person who attends church irregularly, but gives generously on a continuous basis, is, probably, still firmly committed to their local church.[19] However, if someone actively and deliberately cancels their direct debit, even if they keep attending, they are clearly signalling that something has gone wrong.

The second potential benefit of being aware of church giving through online transfer is that church leaderships can express their appreciation. As discussed earlier, people usually have mixed motivations when they give to their local church. But we would hope that people do not give generously because they want the accolades of others. However, that does not mean we should not express our appreciation to those who are giving generously just as we express appreciation to people who exercise a whole range of other ministries in church life. Musicians, Sunday school teachers, welcomers and preachers all receive warm affirmation from the church for their ministry — why not recognise those who are gifted at giving?

Reflection Questions 9.4
1) What do you feel is the most important insight regarding generous giving generated by this chapter?

2) Is there anything you are unsure of or disagree with?

3) What do you feel is the most important insight on generous giving *for your church* generated by this chapter?

4) What else could you do to foster generous giving in your church?

Step 5: Action

As we have highlighted, the practical theological process is not completed when orthodoxy is developed, but when it is implemented. So in this section of each chapter we will be asking you to identify action steps to ensure that good ideas become good practice. Here is a process which you might like to use or adapt for your context:

1) Gather together as a leadership and pray for the discernment of God's wisdom for your church with respect to generous giving.

2) Share together your answers to Reflection Questions 9.4.

3) Individually, write down your answer to the following question: What should our church *do* to foster generous giving? You might come up with up to five suggestions. Try to make your suggestions as specific as possible. For example, rather than just saying "teach more on generous giving," you could suggest something like "Preach a sermon series on God and money during February next year," or "Establish a system whereby regular givers to the church receive a letter of appreciation on behalf of the leadership."

4) Go around the group and have each member suggest one action the church could take to foster generous giving in your church. Write the suggestion on a whiteboard or similar media. If your suggestion has already been made put a tick next to it on the whiteboard and then share your next suggestion.

5) When everyone has shared all of their suggestions, each member in the group is allocated three votes. (You might like to allocate each member three self-adhesive dots for this activity.)

Each member can then use their votes. They can allocate all three votes to the same suggestion or utilise them across a number of suggestions.

6) Tally up the dots and you will have an indication of what, as a leadership team, might be a good action step to take to develop generous giving in your church. Pray again and then decide which action steps you wish to take. Two or three is probably all that you can attempt at one time. Still, keep a record of your suggestions because you may be able to come back to them next year.

Conclusion

Smith, Emerson and Snell suggest that there is sometimes an unspoken agreement between leaders and their congregations: the minister will not speak too much about money and the congregation will give just enough to keep the church running.[20] However, church leadership teams that help their congregations give generously certainly do no harm. In fact, they help disciples to express their gratitude to God and align themselves with God's kingdom work in the world. It enables them to flourish in their spiritual lives as they are set free from slavery to the idolatry of experiences and possessions. There is no need for your church leadership to be apologetic about talking about money. It is probably the biggest issue we face in the Australian Church and we do our people no service to ignore it.

Chapter Endnotes

1. Carol Gan, Michelle Cartwright, Miriam Pepper, Paul Oslington, Nicole Hancock and Ruth Powell, "Faith and Finances: Practices and Attitudes in Australian Churches," *NCLS Occasional Paper 37* (2018).

2. David A. Croteau, *You Mean I Don't Have to Tithe?: A Deconstruction of Tithing and a Reconstruction of Post-Tithe Giving* (Eugene: Pickwick Publications, 2010), 53.

3. LifeWay Research, "Churchgoers Views – Tithing," (2018), http://lifewayresearch.com/wp-content/uploads/2018/05/American-Churchgoers-Tithing-2017.pdf.

4. Andreas J. Köstenberger and David A. Croteau, "Reconstructing a Biblical Model for Giving: A Discussion of Relevant Systematic Issues and New Testament Principles," *Bulletin for Biblical Research 16, no.2* (2006): 237-60.

5. Thomas Schreiner, "7 Reasons Christians Are Not Required to Tithe," The Gospel Coalition, https://www.thegospelcoalition.org/article/7-reasons-christians-not-required-to-tithe/.

6. Adapted from Köstenberger and Croteau, 253.

7. Irenaeus, Against Heresies. Book 4, Chapter 18, Section 2., https://www.newadvent.org/fathers/0103418.htm.

8. Rod Irvine, *Giving Generously: Resourcing Local Church Ministry* (Canberra: Barton Books, 2015), 57.

9. John Wesley, "The Use of Money", *The Works of John Wesley (Vol. 1)* (London: J. Kershaw, 1825) 624-635.

10. Gan et al. 13.

11 Ibid., 20.

12 Bonnie S. Guy and Wesley E. Patton, "The Marketing of Altruistic Causes: Understanding Why People Help," *Journal of Consumer Marketing* 6, no. 1 (1989): 21.

13 Ibid., 25.

14 Dean R. Hoge et al., *Money Matters: Personal Giving in American Churches* (Louisville: Westminster John Knox Press, 1996), 66-72.

15 Irvine, 73-83.

16 Ibid., 88.

17 Ibid., 92.

18 Adapted from Church Growth Services, "Seven Keys to Cultivating Generosity at Your Church," https://churchgrowthservices.com/resources/seven-keys-to-cultivating-biblical-stewardship-at-your-church/.

19 The scenario where a person is committed financially to a church, but not to personal relationship with people in the church is problematic. This is just one more complex issue for local church leaderships to wrestle with and respond to pastorally!

20 Christian Smith, Michael O. Emerson, and Patricia Snell, *Passing the Plate: Why American Christians Don't Give Away More Money* (Oxford: Oxford University Press, 2008), 72.

Conclusion

There is a church, and no one knows its name. I mean, the people who are members of that church know its name, and the people in the community that it serves know its name. But it's not famous. It doesn't make it on to Christian television. There never has been, nor will there ever be, a book written about it, let alone a story about it on a Current Affair. Most people in the world will never know it exists, or what it does.

But it is a supernatural phenomenon. People just don't realise it.

At its heart is a vision of the kingdom of God, and what God is doing in the world. There is a quiet determination to live kingdom shaped lives in this kingdom shaped church. It only grasps the nature of the kingdom partially, and it is only occasionally that those in the church experience a powerful taste of what the consummated kingdom will be like. But it does happen. On those occasions the members of the church find a quiet satisfied smile on their face and a peace in their heart. And they say to one another, "God was at work today." Others have a tear in their eye, and just nod and smile. Sometimes words are neither needed nor adequate…

In a world where lots of people are hope-less, this church is hope-full. Sure, there are problems and issues that emerge in the church, but hope is never extinguished. The light might grow dim, but it always burns. There is always the calm assurance that if Jesus rose from the dead anything is possible. He is indeed a king like no other for a kingdom like no other.

This hopefulness is enhanced by the church's sense of community. People from outside the church look on at the way these disciples love one another, and although they won't say it, they desperately want to be part of what is going on. The people in the church are not always aware of just how powerful and attractive their simple acts of community commitment are. They think it is just normal to love one another. They think this is just the way life is. But those looking in know that these crazy Christians have something really special going on.

But even though they have a strong sense of community, they are not a "holy huddle." They often share meals together with one another, but also with others who do not belong to their community. They are also actively involved in good things that other community groups are doing as well. You often see these people involved in Meals on Wheels, sports clubs, school P&Cs, clean up Australia day. They are often the most valued employees in their workplaces. They are the "salt of the earth."

A visitor to the Sunday worship service might wonder where the leaders are. There are no special car parks in the parking lot, no big corner offices. The leaders, whoever they are, just seem to blend in with everyone else. What the visitor can't see, in fact what most of the people in the church don't see, is the sense of responsibility that rests heavy on the shoulders of the leaders. They, more than anyone, are steeped in this church's vision of the kingdom and embody its determination to achieve its kingdom purposes through their practice of its kingdom values in their leadership. The responsibility of leading this no-name church is a difficult blessing. It is exciting to be called to this role, but these leaders realise the power they have is dangerous stuff. In fact, they spend most of their time try to give it away!

The people in this church have a fundamentally countercultural predisposition. They believe in the supernatural. Although God is not physically visible, they live as though God is with them all the time, alive to his presence and priority in all they do. They share stories about how God is "working" in their lives, even though they can't physically see, touch or hear God. Their lives are shaped by God's word to them in Scripture – and they have this annoying habit of stopping all the time and talking to God. Their faith is not dead – it is vibrant.

Although people in this church know that God is at work in them and through them achieving his purposes for the world throughout the week, the visitor would sense there is a special sense God is at work amongst his people as they gather for worship. Extra special things happen when the church gathers on Sundays. People catch fresh glimpses of God and his kingdom and respond authentically. They make decisions and take big steps forward in their faith. They become more wholehearted in their devotion to God and their lives are re-formed, made ready for the great wedding feast when Christ comes again.

Another thing that might be invisible to a visitor is the radical transformation of human lives that is going on in this church. During the course of the week various members are meeting together and helping each other to flourish and more fully submit to Jesus' reign. Sometimes it happens when individuals are reading their Bibles and praying. Sometimes it happens when people meet one on one. Sometimes it happens in groups. Sometimes it happens on mission trips. Sometimes there are remarkable intergenerational relationships like of which exist nowhere else in society. Old and young, loving and learning to be like Jesus together.

In fact the visitor might conclude that this church is obsessed with the younger generation. The church people go out of their way to accommodate young people and encourage them. They clearly think children and young people are really, really, really important. And everybody seems to be related. Children call older people in the congregation "uncle" and "auntie" even when they actually aren't their uncles or aunties! There is an old saying that it takes a village to raise a child. Well, this is a village and you can just see the children and young people flourishing before your eyes.

This church is making a serious contribution to the world. They give money to support a wide range of activities that bring no direct benefit to them. The visitor might be prompted to ask, "Who pays for all this?" The church employs people, maintains this community facility and gives generously to the poor. Do they get government funding? No. "It's the people in the church to give the money to make this happen." Really? Why?

Why?

Why does any of this happen? Why are these people so weird? It's like the people from this church are from another planet. Or is it another kingdom?

Appendix 1
Supplementary Questions

Chapter 1 Kingdom Aligned Vision
Supplementary Reflection questions 1.1

Understanding the history of your church's vision statements will enable you to more fully understand the context in which you currently operate:

1) Look back over previous vision statements

    a) What are the recurrent words/themes?

    b) Which words/themes have changed?

    c) What do the elements which have stayed the same or changed tell you about the trajectory and priorities of your church?

2) In relation to your current vision statement?

    a) When was this developed?

    b) By whom?

    c) What prompted this work?

    d) What were the key aspects of your church's context to which this statement responded?

    e) What has changed/stayed the same since its development?

Supplementary Reflection Questions 1.2

1) Jesus' life and ministry as they are portrayed in the Gospels are full of kingdom life. Some churches follow a lectionary pattern which ensures that there is always a Gospel reading during their worship to focus their attention on this.

a) How often and in what ways is your congregation encouraged to fix their sights on Jesus' kingdom life and ministry?

2) People visiting our churches should experience a foretaste of the kingdom

   a) Which features of kingdom life does your church best reflect?

   b) Which features of kingdom life represent the greatest challenge to your church?

3) In what ways does your church look ahead to the fulfilment of the kingdom?

   a) Is your language concerning death, resurrection, heaven, Christ's return and the fulfilment of his kingdom scripturally sound and consistent?

4) Does your church's hopefulness embrace the redemption of persons, community and creation?

   a) How does your language/teaching encompass each of these dimensions?

   b) In what ways does this hopefulness stir your congregation to action?

Supplementary Reflection Questions 1.3

1) Spend some time with a sample of different people (young and old, male and female, young and mature in faith) from your congregation.

   a) What do they understand about the nature of Christian hope?

   b) How do they relate your church's vision statement to this?

   c) What do they know of how your church is planning to move towards this vision?

   d) Can they identify a way in which they can participate in this?

Supplementary Reflection Questions 1.4

1) In discerning a focused vision for your church, discuss

   a) how God is already at work in your context

b) the particular opportunities and challenges associated with your context

c) your church's DNA (history, challenges etc)

d) the skills, experience and passions of your leaders and people

e) the Spirit's leading through Scripture, prayer or prophecy

Chapter 2 Strong Community
Supplementary Reflection questions 2.1

1) How are each of these terms expressed in your church context?

   a) Authenticity

   b) Hospitality

   c) Relational intentionality

   d) Loving relationships

   e) Connection with others

   f) A sense of belonging

   g) Intentional and welcoming inclusion

   h) Participation in the congregation

   i) Welcoming new people

Supplementary Reflection questions 2.2

1) How might you engage with the "everyday" activities recorded in Acts 2:42, 46-47a, to encourage a sense of belonging and community in your church?

2) What forms of scriptural language do you use to describe the community of your church and what do these mean to you?

3) How could you recognise and encourage the practice of these scriptural "one anothers"?

4) How do you celebrate the various forms of belonging to your church community?

Supplementary Reflection Questions 2.3

1) Reflect on the dimensions of community highlighted by McMillan and Chavis.

a) What are some of the shared values, beliefs and rituals which enable of sense of belonging for your church community?

b) Which kinds of congregational members are most likely to experience frequent and meaningful connection with one another?

c) Which kinds of congregational members are most likely to miss out on the experience of frequent and meaningful connection with one another?

d) What channels of communication are open to your congregation to influence the vision, ministry and mission of your church?

e) When and how are there opportunities to share stories about faith and community?

Supplementary Reflection Questions 2.4

1) Are there groups within your church which are underrepresented in current expressions of community (singles, seniors, persons with disability, men or women)? What barriers do they face?

2) Do you think a sense of community has increased or decreased for people in your church over time (one year, five years, twenty years), and what might have contributed to this change?

Chapter 3 Outward Focus
Supplementary Reflection Questions 3.1

1) What evangelistic programs has the church used over the years? How did they go?

2) When and how do you practice awareness of your local, national and global community (e.g., through crisis fund raising or intercessory prayer)?

Supplementary Reflection Questions 3.2

1) There are three major dimensions which come through this engagement with Scripture regarding outward focus:

a) Word and deed

b) Being and going

c) Hospitality

2) How are these expressed by your church and its congregational members?

3) Where does the balance usually fall and does this require attention?

Supplementary Reflection Questions 3.3
1) A vibrant faith (see Chapter 5) is a powerful motivator for sharing the blessings of salvation. How might you encourage your congregation to "wear their heart (for God) on their sleeve"?

2) Is your church more attractional or incarnational in its approach to evangelism?

3) Talk with your congregation about the specific fears they might face in inviting people to explore the gospel. How might you help them overcome these barriers?

4) How might you encourage your congregation to relate their everyday work to the work of the kingdom?

Supplementary Reflection Questions 3.4
1) Do your church facilities speak of welcome and hospitality to those who visit?

- Take a tour of your facilities with someone in a wheelchair and with a sensory or neurological form of difference. What obstacles or barriers might they experience?

2) What forms of hospitality are already being offered by your church as a whole or on an individual basis?

- Where does your emphasis tend to fall and, if needed, how might the weaker elements be strengthened?

3) In your 'gathered' form, how is your church proclaiming the gospel of the kingdom?

4) In your 'scattered' form, what more could your church do to support your attendees on their frontlines for the sake of the gospel?

Chapter 4 Empowering Leadership
Supplementary Reflection questions 4.1
1) Taking a broad approach, identify as many "leaders" as possible within your church

    a) Who is responsibly exercising their own power in contributing to your church's vision – and who are they encouraging/influencing/empowering? (Remember to look across age groups, genders and personality types).

    b) Would their ministry benefit from some form of church recognition or endorsement?

2) Are there areas of ministry or mission which are important to your church's vision which are lacking leadership? How might you address this?

Supplementary Reflection Questions 4.2
1) In what ways does your church recognise and celebrate Jesus' victorious power?

2) Has there been any history of power abuse in your church? Has there been healing for those effected or are the consequences still being felt?

3) How can you encourage your church to provide support and encouragement for those in leadership without an unhealthy focus or dependence on them?

Supplementary Reflection Questions 4.3
1) Leadership needs to be both effective and relational. Such standards are highly complex and many outcomes are beyond the control of leaders – and yet failing to assess and evaluate our leadership is also unhelpful.

    a) How do/could you measure the effectiveness of your leadership in your various spheres of influence?

      b) How do/could you measure the relational quality of your leadership?

  2) What forms of support and accountability are in place for those in leadership in your church?

Supplementary Reflection Questions 4.4

1) In what ways does the term "servant" change the ways in which you lead your church?

2) In what ways does the term "empowering" change the ways in which you lead your church?

3) How might you empower more of your congregation to achieve kingdom ends by kingdom means?

Chapter 5 Vibrant Faith

Supplementary Reflection Questions 5.1

1) What does vibrant faith look like for you? Write out a definition and share it with one another.

2) Share stories of how God has developed vibrant faith in your life. What are the commonalities and differences between your stories?

Supplementary Reflection Questions 5.2

1) Enthusiasm and zeal may be expressed in different ways by different people.

    a) Which members of your congregation come to mind when you consider these terms?

    b) How do they express their enthusiasm or zeal for God?

2) Which members of your congregation come to mind when you consider the fruit of the Spirit? Which fruit do they exemplify?

3) Which members of your congregation come to mind when you consider the gifts of the Spirit? Which gifts do they practice for the good of your church?

4) How could you empower these people to tell their stories and empower others?

Supplementary Reflection Questions 5.3
1) What terms would you use to describe the culture of your church in relation to
   a) Prayer?
   b) Bible reading?
   c) Story sharing?
2) Do these terms reflect long term culture or has something changed – for better or worse?
3) What might have contributed to any such changes – and what can you learn from these?

Supplementary Reflection Questions 5.4
1) Work your way through the suggestions raised by Silverzweig and Allen's model of cultural change. As you prepare to act on some of these
   a) Identify key people who exemplify the key features of the culture you want to encourage. (Try to think beyond the usual suspects!)
   b) How might you empower them to influence others?

Chapter 6 Inspiring Worship
Supplementary Reflection Questions 6.1
1) Consider some of the dimensions of your church's worship
   a) Is continuity with your faith tradition a high priority, or are you more committed to relevance to your surrounding culture? Do you seek to balance these, or does one or the other tend to predominate in your choices of hymns/songs, forms of prayer, and other elements of worship?
   b) Do your services generally reflect a concern for good planning and order or is spontaneity expected and welcomed?
   c) How much of your worship is "passive" and how much and in what ways do people actively participate?

2) Identify if and when there have been any changes to your church's form of corporate worship. What prompted these and how were they received?

Supplementary Reflection Questions 6.2
1) Make a list of the various components of your worship service (e.g. singing, Bible reading, ministry time etc.). How authentic are these expressions? How participative are they?
2) How much is our worship service shaped intentionally? How much is just habit?

Supplementary Reflection Questions 6.3
1) Give your church a score out of 10 for each of the following vital aspects of church worship:

   a) A sense of God's presence

   b) Awe or mystery

   c) Joy

   d) Growth in understanding of God

   e) Preaching that is helpful to everyday life

2) How "contemporary" is the music in your church service? Do you think this is an important issue with respect to attracting young people?

Supplementary Reflection Questions 6.4
1) Where are we expecting to meet God and experience the kingdom in our worship services?
2) What are we doing to make sure this happens?

Chapter 7 Intentional Discipleship
Supplementary Reflection Questions 7.1
1) The other terms raised by research into congregational forms of discipleship (see introduction) include:

   a) Transforming discipleship

   b) Maturation of believers

c) Intentional faith development
  d) Learning and growing in community
  e) Holistic small groups

Which of these terms "fit" with your sense of discipleship for your congregation? Why?

Supplementary Reflection Questions 7.2
1) What struck you most about Jesus' form of discipleship?
2) At what stage in the discipleship journey does your church raise the issue of "counting the cost" of discipleship and how?
3) In what ways do you address self-denial?
4) How does your church celebrate the empowerment of the Holy Spirit for discipleship?
5) How is baptism (whatever form you practice) recognised as part of the discipleship process?
6) At each level (whole church, small groups, one on one) what forms of discipleship are currently in use?

Supplementary Reflection Questions 7.3
1) With what forms of digital discipleship are members of your congregation engaging and how does this vary across their various demographic groupings?
2) In what ways might your church harness these resources and the learning people are gaining from them?
3) What proportions of your congregation belong to each of the four stages of growth outlined by the Reveal research? And what might this mean for the focus of your discipleship strategies?
4) How are you addressing the need for whole life discipleship which prepares people to follow Jesus and make disciples on their frontlines?

5) How have short-term mission trips contributed to the discipleship of your congregation in the past and what opportunities might there be for these in the future?

Supplementary Reflection Questions 7.4
1) What is the "discipleship plan" for your church? If Jesus was to come back and ask you how you were fulfilling his commission, what would you point to?

2) When you were a young Christian, how were you discipled? How are you discipled now?

Chapter 8 Caring for the Young
Supplementary Reflection Questions 8.1
1) Meet a young person aged 15-29 for coffee or lunch. Invite them to share their general perception of your church and the way young people are welcomed, included and encouraged.

2) The inclusion of children in your worship services may range from complete to none. Where along this spectrum do you fall and what are the advantages and disadvantages of your approach?

3) How do you practice multi-generational discipleship?

Supplementary Reflection Questions 8.2
1) How does your church help parents disciple their children?

2) What symbols of redemption (monuments or rituals) does your church have that would help pass faith to the next generation?

3) How welcome do children feel in your church services? How do you know?

Supplementary Reflection Questions 8.3
1) Meaningful intergenerational relationships are crucial to helping young people in church communities. How many intergenerational relationships do you as leaders have with younger people in your church?

2) What can be done to foster more of these relationships in your church?

Supplementary Reflection Questions 8.4
1) How do you go about recognising and promoting leadership among young people?
2) In what ways are young people's concerns and convictions listened to and included in decisions about your church's vision, ministry and mission?
3) Go through the six core commitments identified by the Fuller youth Institute. What evidence do you have that these are observable in your church?

Chapter 9 Generous Giving
Supplementary Reflection Questions 9.1
1) Does, or has the church ever, had a "stewardship" program? How effective was it?

Supplementary Reflection Questions 9.2
1) What is your understanding and approach to the concept of tithing?
2) How do/might you celebrate generous giving as a church or with generous individuals?

Supplementary Reflection Questions 9.3
1) How might you apply each of the principles of encouraging generous philanthropy to church giving?
2) How do you rate your church's financial transparency and the inclusion of the congregation in budgeting and setting financial priorities? How could you improve these?
3) In what ways do you encourage your congregation to be committed givers to both regular ministry needs and special projects?

Supplementary Reflection Questions 9.4

1) When will you next be teaching on money, stewardship and generous giving? When could you schedule this into your preaching calendar (by topic or appropriate biblical text)?

2) How might you better help people see the connections between their giving and the kingdom aligned vision towards which you are working together?

3) When and how might it be appropriate to (privately) thank specific givers?

4) When and how do you report your financial status to your congregation? Would they (and their giving) benefit from more regular updates?

5) How are you incorporating the acknowledgement of online giving into your "offering time"

Appendix 2
What is "Vibrant" Faith?

In their meta-analysis of research into church vitality, Powell et al. identify a dimension called "Spirituality."[1] They do this because several research projects into church vitality identify that the spirituality in vital churches is passionate,[2] growing,[3] and alive.[4]

But according to The Natural Church Development (NCD) research, a key measure of vitality which they call "Passionate Spirituality," is related to "the degree to which faith is actually lived out with commitment, passion and enthusiasm."[5] The statements associated with this measure include:

- I experience God's work in my life
- I experience the transforming influences faith has in the different areas of my life (profession, family, spare time, etc)
- I often tell other Christians when I have experienced something from God
- Times of prayer are an inspiring experience for me
- I know that other church members pray for me regularly
- I enjoy reading the Bible on my own
- The Bible is a powerful guide for me in the decisions of everyday life
- I am enthusiastic about our church
- I firmly believe that God will act even more powerfully in our church in coming years
- Our leaders are spiritual examples to me.

Other research[6] indicates that congregants in healthy churches in the United States:

- Believe their spiritual needs were met by their congregations

- Spent at least a few times per week in devotional activities
- Are growing in their faith
- Highly value Bible study and prayer.

The NCLS core quality, "An Alive and Growing Faith," which Powell et al. categorise under the heading "Spirituality" in their meta-analysis,[7] is related to the following:

- Importance of God: how important respondents believe God is to them
- Faith commitment: whether respondents have experienced a moment of faith commitment or whether their commitment grew gradually
- Private devotional activity: whether and how often respondents spend time in private devotions (prayer or Bible reading)
- Growth in faith: whether, and to what extent, attenders believe that their faith has grown in the past year.[8]

The meta-analysis also had a separate feature they call "prayer."[9] It refers to God-centred prayer, Spiritual disciplines, contemplation and prayerful dependence.

As you read through these statements, we hope you agree that it is sensible to combine these two features of vital churches as "Vibrant Faith" rather than separately as "Spirituality" and "Prayer." We think this single term captures what is actually being identified in these two features. We define Vibrant Faith as:

> Knowing and trusting God more and more through prayer and Bible reading and their day-to-day experience of participating in his kingdom.

People in vital churches are getting to "know" God and trust him more and more through prayer and Bible reading and their day-to-day experience of participating in his kingdom.

Chapter Endnotes

1. Ruth Powell et al., "Models of Church Vitality: A Literature Review," *NCLS Occasional Paper* 39 (2019).

2. Christian Schwarz, *Natural Church Development* (Emmelsbull: C. and P. Publishing, 1996), 28-29.

3. Cynthia Woolever and Deborah Bruce, *Beyond the Ordinary: Ten Strengths of Us Congregations* (Louisville: Westminster John Knox Press, 2004), 16.

4. Ruth Powell et al., *Enriching Church Life*, 2nd ed. (Saint Mary's: Mirrabooka Press & NCLS Research, 2012), 19.

5. Christian A. Schwarz, *Natural Church Development: A Guide to Eight Essential Qualities of Healthy Churches (7th Updated and Revised Edition)* (St. Charles: Churchsmart Resources, 2006).

6. Woolever and Bruce, 16.

7. Powell et al., "Models of Church Vitality: A Literature Review."

8. Powell et al., *Enriching Church Life*, 12.

9. Powell et al., "Models of Church Vitality: A Literature Review," 14.

About the Authors

IAN HUSSEY was a pastor for 17 years before becoming a lecturer at Malyon Theological College, Brisbane, Australia in 2011. He teaches in the area of ministry and practice and also serves as the Regional Minister for the Metro Central region of Queensland Baptists.

ANNE KLOSE is a pastoral supervisor, theologian and church historian and lectures in the area of Baptist distinctives and spiritual formation at Malyon Theological College. She has served on the Board of Queensland Baptists and continues to research and write in the area of Baptist ecclesiology.

www.ingramcontent.com/pod-product-compliance
Lightning Source LLC
Chambersburg PA
CBHW070729020526
44107CB00077B/2186